BISHOP SARAPION'S
PRAYER-BOOK

BISHOP SARAPION'S
PRAYER-BOOK

AN EGYPTIAN SACRAMENTARY DATED PROBABLY
ABOUT A.D. 350–356

With Introduction, Notes, and Indices

BY

JOHN WORDSWORTH, D.D.

BISHOP OF SALISBURY

ARCHON BOOKS
Hamden, Connecticut
1964

First published 1899
by the Society for Promoting Christian Knowledge
(Translations of Christian Literature, Series III,
Liturgical Texts)

Reprinted 1964
from the Second Edition, Revised, 1923

Printed in The United States of America

64866

CONTENTS

6 CONTENTS

BISHOP SARAPION'S PRAYER-BOOK

INTRODUCTION

§ 1. *Date and importance of the Book. Description of the MS.*

The little book which came quietly into our hands in the first weeks of the year 1899, as part of a small fasciculus of the well-known Leipzig series of *Texte und Untersuchungen*,[1] is one of the most important additions to early Christian Literature made in a century which has been specially favoured in regard to discoveries of this kind. It is a Liturgical document of first-rate importance. In the first place, we know its approximate date and authorship, and the country to which it belongs. It is clearly

---

[1] *Altchristliche Liturgische Stücke aus der Kirche Aegyptens nebst einem dogmatischen Brief des Bischofs Serapion von Thmuis*, von Georg Wobbermin, Dr. Phil., Lic. Theol., in *Texte und Untersuchungen*, neue Folge, II. 3b. Leipzig, 1899, price 2s. It was first printed in *Trudy*, the Journal of the Ecclesiastical Academy of Kieff in 1894. Canon Brightman's edition in *J. of Th. Studies*, Oct. 1899 and Jan. 1900, must be consulted by all advanced students.

Egyptian, and of about the middle of the fourth century, and there seems no sufficient reason to doubt that it is, in whole or in part, the Prayer-book compiled or composed by Sarapion, Bishop of Thmuis, the friend and contemporary of St. Antony and St. Athanasius. It is therefore superior as a historical document to those three books with which it is at once natural to compare it—the *Teaching of the Apostles*, the *Canons of Hippolytus*, and the *Liturgy of the Apostolic Constitutions*, commonly called the *Clementine Liturgy*. Their authorship, date, and origin, and in the case of the second its text, are matters of laborious inference, and capable of lengthy discussion. Personally, I incline to accept the date generally given to the *Teaching of the Apostles*, and should assign it to the first half of the second century, with, of course, a possible earlier date for portions of it. The *Canons of Hippolytus*, painfully reconstructed from the Arabic version of a Coptic version of a lost Greek book, are believed, with probability, to represent Roman practice about the beginning of the third century. The eighth book of the *Constitutions*, as seems to have been proved, is an edition of the Antiochene Liturgy by the same remarkable but unknown author, to whom we owe the compilation of the rest of that volume and the interpolation of the genuine and the creation of the false Ignatius.[1] It is, like Sarapion, a document of the fourth century, but one prejudiced by the shadow in which its author moved, and the heretical bias by which he was in some degree actuated.[2]

The MS. in which Sarapion's Liturgy is contained, is no. 149 of the Lavra Monastery of Mount Athos, apparently of the eleventh century, and consists (according to the editor Dr. George Wobbermin's careful description) of 149 leaves, 18·2 centimetres × 14 centimetres (about $7\frac{1}{8}$ × $5\frac{1}{2}$ inches) in dimensions. It contains a *Confession concerning the Orthodox Faith* by " Euthalius, Bishop of Sulké " (Σούλκης); the letter of St. Athanasius to the Philosopher Maximus (*P. Gr.*, xxvi. 1086) ; then from fol. 7 *verso* to 24 *verso* the thirty Prayers here

---

[1] See the admirable summary of the arguments on these points in the *Introduction* (pp. xvii—xlvii) to Rev. F. E. Brightman's *Liturgies Eastern and Western*, vol. i., Oxford 1896. I have throughout quoted the Eastern Liturgies by the pages of this book. I have also profited largely by personal intercourse with Mr. Brightman, who has been further good enough to read through the version of the Prayers printed below, and to criticize it in a most helpful manner, besides making suggestions as to the import of many of the prayers.

[2] He was not an Arian, but had Subordinationist tendencies, and he denied our Lord's human soul : *cp.* Brightman, p. xxviii. The date is uncertain, but it may be assigned to 350—400, possibly *circa* 380.

translated, and a dogmatic letter *Concerning Father and Son ;* and lastly, pieces of the Septuagint, Job, with the Prologue of Polychronius, Wisdom of Jesus son of Sirach, Proverbs of Solomon (preceded by their ὑπόθεσις), Ecclesiastes, and the Song of Songs.

The portion with which we are concerned is thus confined to eighteen leaves of the MS., of which the last four (21 *recto* to 24 *verso*) contain the dogmatic treatise already referred to, in the form of a letter to a brother or near relation of the author, but without any name or historical indication being given.

§ 2. *Personality and Character of Sarapion of Thmuis. His orthodoxy in regard to the Doctrine of the holy Spirit. Question of the Doxology.*

The name Sarapion is found in the entries before the first and fifteenth prayers, in the first of which he is called " Bishop Sarapion," in the second "Sarapion, Bishop of Thmuis." Here we are on historical ground, since a Bishop of this name and of this see has long been known to Church historians. Thmuis is a town in Lower Egypt, in the Delta between the Mendesian and Tanitic branches of the Nile, near Lake Menzaleh, and not far south of Mendes. Its ruins are now shown at Tmey-el-Amdid, some five miles east of the railway between Mansûra and Abû Kebîr. It is mentioned by Herodotus, ii. 166. The name is said to be derived from Thmu, the he-goat, worshipped here and at Mendes, with which city it was in close relation. (*Cp.* St. Jerome, *in Isaiam,* lib. xiii. cap. xlvi. 1, and *in Jovinian.* ii. 5.) There is, it may be remarked, no direct reference in these prayers to idolatry ; but there are references to "Satanic faults" and "energies" on one side, and frequent prayers for the grace of "cleanness" on the other, which may be tacit allusions to the base Egyptian nature-worship of the neighbourhood. Evil spirits are also mentioned, and there is a contrast between false and true worship in no. 9, "those that are worse" being opposed to "the God of truth," and something like it in no. 8.

The name Sarapion, or (as it is usually but perhaps less correctly spelt) Serapion, is a common one, being derived from the favourite deity of later Egyptian mythology, a combination of Osiris and Apis. No less than sixteen persons bearing the name are described in the *Dictionary of Christian Biography.* Our Bishop is known as a saint and a literary man, bearing the title Scholasticus to distinguish him from others, and having a festival on 21st March. He was an intimate friend of the great Athanasius, and of his friend the hermit Antony.

His relation to Antony was so close that the
latter specially made him the confidant of his
visions. One in particular is mentioned in this
connection (*Vita Antonii*, 82), which presaged
the Arian irruption into Egypt and the profan-
ation of the Church of Alexandria. Antony, on
his death, which took place (shortly before the
inroad of Arianism) early in the year 356, desired
his disciples to bury his body and to keep the
place concealed, that it might not be exhibited
in houses, as the bad custom then was ; and
then he disposed of his clothing. "Divide my
garments" (he said). "Give one sheepskin cloak
to Athanasius the Bishop, and the pallium on
which I lay, which he gave me new, and which
has grown old with my use ; and give the other
sheepskin cloak to Sarapion the Bishop : and
do you keep my shirt of goats' hair. And now
farewell, children. Antony goeth hence, and is
no longer with you" (*ibid.* 91). The persecution
which followed began in February 356, and
lasted till the death of Constantius and the
accession of Julian in 361. It is no doubt to
this epoch that we must assign the " Confession "
of Sarapion, of which St. Jerome speaks (*De
viris illustribus*, 99) as " sub Constantio principe."
For Constantius did not succeed to power in
Egypt till after the death of Constans in 350,

and did not interfere violently on behalf of
Arianism in that country till early in the year
356. It seems natural to suppose that the
Liturgical work of Sarapion would fall in the
time of peace which preceded A.D. 356. But
the very short and reserved prayer for " rulers "
in 27 is suitable to the reign of Constantius, so
that I incline to a date 350—356. *Cp.* § 4, p. 26.

St. Jerome also tells us that Sarapion wrote
an excellent treatise against the Manicheans,
and one on the titles of the Psalms, as well as
useful Epistles to various persons. The Book
on the Psalms is lost, but the treatise against
the Manicheans still exists, and is of considerable length when its fragments are pieced
together.[1]

---

[1] The main collection of Sarapion's works will be found
in Migne's *Patrologia Græca*, vol. xl. 899 foll. They
consist of the book *Against the Manicheans, Letter to the
Bishop Eudoxius, Letter to the Solitaries* (πρὸς μονάζοντας).
Dr. Wobbermin points out, after Brinkmann, that the
book against the Manicheans is to be enlarged by the
addition of five fragments printed in the anti-Manichean
treatise of Titus of Bostra, which come in between Migne
921 c. τῇ ἀρχῇ τῶν and τῆς πονηρίας ἱστῶν. They are Titus,
ed. Lagarde, 1859 (1) 72, 29—75, 25 ; (2) 69, 29—72, 29 ; (3)
78, 19—79, 37 ; (4) 75, 25—78, 19 ; (5) 79, 37—103, 16. A
lacuna still exists after No. 2. A small fragment discovered
by Cardinal Pitra is in one of Brinkmann's discoveries,
but he has added a few others, one in Greek from Cod.
Coislin. 279, and three in Syriac from Cod. Add. Mus. Brit.
12,156. The Greek fragment shows that as many as
twenty-three letters (at least) of Sarapion's were at one

Sarapion was himself a letter writer to a considerable extent, though the larger number of his letters are lost. But he will always be particularly known to theologians, as the recipient of five important letters from St. Athanasius, which bear witness, among other things, to the high regard and frequent intercourse which existed between them. The first describes the death of Arius, "refuting the notion that he had died in Church communion, by an account of his death, the details of which Athanasius had learned from his Presbyter Macarius, while he himself was resident at Trier." [1] It was written apparently in 358. The four dogmatic and controversial letters also belong, it would seem, to the same year, and followed in the line of Athanasius' *Orations*, of which the second letter briefly repeats the teaching, while the others, says Dr. Bright, "were directed against a theory then reported to him by Sarapion as springing up, afterwards known as Macedonianism ; which,

time extant. The Syriac extracts are from a Homily on Virginity and a Letter to Confessors, and a short dogmatic fragment.

[1] See W. Bright, *Life of St. Athanasius*, prefixed to the Oxford edition of the *Orations against the Arians*, p. lxvii, 1873. The letter is simply addressed "To Sarapion the brother." It will be found in Migne, *P. Gr.* xxv. 685—690.

abandoning the Arian position in regard to the Son, strove, with singular inconsistency, to retain it in regard to the Spirit, whom it declared to be neither a Divine Person nor a Divine Attribute, but a ministering creature, differing only in degree from the angels." [1]

Shortly after the receipt of these letters must fall the " Confession " of Sarapion, for we find that, in the year 359, the Council of Seleucia was attended by an Acacian Bishop Ptolemaeus, who is described as " Bishop of Thmuis." It is natural to conjecture, that, just as George of Cappadocia was intruded into the see of Athanasius, so Ptolemaeus was intruded into that of Sarapion. Acacius was the scheming head of an offshoot of Arianism, and had at this period great influence with Constantius. We do not know whether Sarapion died in prison or in exile, or survived to welcome back his friend.

St. Athanasius' Epistles to Sarapion seem to be, to a great extent, summaries or repetitions of arguments used by him elsewhere; but the last contains a careful discussion of the " blasphemy against the Holy Ghost " (St. Matt. xii.

---

[1] Bright, *l. c.*, p. lxxiv.   These four letters are in Migne, *P. Gr.* xxvi. 529—676 ; they are addressed " To Sarapion, Bishop of Thmuis," and they mention that they are written from the retreat in the desert.

31), which seems newly thought out, and was written at the special request of his correspondent. Where Sarapion is personally addressed it is with affection and even deference, as a friend "beloved and longed for," whose judgment is respected. I can see no evidence that Athanasius suspected him of any heretical bias. A careless reader might possibly think so from the language of the writer, which suddenly changes from "they" to "you," and continues to refute the heretics who are in view, whether Arians or others, as if he were writing directly to them (*Ep.* i. 3).

It is true that the personality of the holy Spirit is not so distinctly brought out in this collection containing Sarapion's prayers, as we might have expected if they had been composed in post-Macedonian times. The definite article is rarely used (τὸ πνεῦμα), and therefore it is not introduced into my version; and personal action is rarely attributed to the third Person of the Blessed Trinity. It is, however, attributed to Him in 1, "May the Lord Jesus speak in us and holy Spirit, and hymn thee through us"; and 10, "Let thy holy Word accompany him, let thy holy Spirit be with him, scaring away and driving off every temptation" (*cp.* 19).

The form of the doxology which comes

regularly at the end of each prayer is very
noticeable in this connection.   It is an ascription
of glory and strength *to* God the Father, *through*
His only-begotten Son, *in* (the) holy Spirit.[1]
This is an archaic form which has also been
preserved in certain parts of the Liturgy in the
Apostolic Constitutions, e. g. vii. 45 (Prayer of
one newly baptized), and 48 (Evening Prayer) ;
viii. 5 (Ordination of a Bishop) ; 6 (Blessing of
Catechumens = Brightman, p. 5) ; 8 (for those
expecting Baptism = p. 7) ; 9 (for Penitents = p.
9 ;) 11 (for the Faithful = p. 13).   But the Prayers
in the latter part of the Eighth Book of the *Constitutions* (= pp. 23, 24, 26, 27), and in the other
Liturgies, generally have an ascription of glory
to the Son, and generally also *to* Him *with* the
holy Spirit.   This is the case even in the *Canons
of Hippolytus*, which have in many points preserved an archaic form, in the prayers at the
ordination of a Bishop (18) and Deacon (42),
and the ministry of Chrism (138), which run,
"through whom to thee with Him and the holy
Spirit."

The learned reader will be aware that the use
of the two forms of doxology gave rise to a
question out of which grew the book of St.

[1] So also in 1 C : "we have invoked thee, the uncreated,
through the only-begotten in holy Spirit."

B

Basil *on the holy Spirit* (see *de Sp. Sanct. ad Amphilochium*, I. 3). The Macedonians, or Pneumatomachi (*i. e.* enemies of the Spirit), attached much importance to the form which is used by Sarapion and in the *Apostolic Constitutions*, which they misinterpreted as implying that the Son was a subordinate agent and the holy Spirit a place. St. Basil's book is in fact very largely a treatise on the use of the prepositions *of* and *through*, *with* and *in*, in regard to the different persons of the Blessed Trinity. St. Basil, of course, proves that they may all be used in a proper and orthodox manner, and that they afford no ground to the heretics for their exaggerated theories of subordination. It is in fact clear that glory to God *through* Jesus Christ is a New Testament usage, as in the Epistle of St. Jude, verse 25, and probably 1 Pet. iv. 11 ; *cp.* 1 Cor. viii. 6 (quoted by Aetius). But it is also clear that we can say of God the Father, "*from* whom and *through* whom and *to* whom are all things" (Rom. xi. 36, *l. c.* v. 7). As to the use of *in* in regard to the holy Spirit, he shows that this is not less honourable than *with* (xxv. 58 foll.). His quotations from early writers, Clement of Rome, Irenaeus, Dionysius of Rome, Dionysius of Alexandria, and Eusebius of Cæsarea, are specially interesting as proving

the early use of doxologies or similar forms implying the consubstantiality of the holy Spirit
(xxix. 72). His own conclusion is that it is
more fitting to use the phrase "with whom"
in doxologies, and "through whom" in thanksgivings (vii. 16). This is no doubt a reasonable
usage—as bringing out our Lord's mediatorial
power in regard to the benefits we receive from
God—but it cannot be said to be a test of
orthodoxy, or the reverse.

The final clause of Sarapion's doxology "in
holy Spirit" is not perfectly easy of interpretation, but I believe that it means "in the unity
of the holy Spirit," so that we might paraphrase
"to the Father through the Son, bound as they
are together by the holy Spirit." In any case
there seems no reason to think that this doxology
would have been criticized by St. Athanasius,
who, in his very full analysis of Scriptural usage,
insists on the presence of the definite article
(*the* Spirit), when some other epithet or attribute
of divinity (*e.g.* holy) was not present, but not
otherwise. (See *Epist. ad Serap.* i. 4.)

This conclusion naturally leads us on to ask
another question.

§ 3. *Was Sarapion author of the Letter "Concerning Father and Son"?*

This Letter, which follows immediately on the

Prayers, does not bear any name, and has no special points of contact as regards style with the Prayers, while it is unlike the style of the Treatise against the Manicheans. Indeed Canon J. Armitage Robinson (whose opinion on such a point is valuable) thinks that it is impossible for them to be by the same author. Without venturing so absolute an opinion, I would notice certain points which made me hesitate to accept Dr. Wobbermin's opinion that Sarapion is the author of the Letter, which I was first inclined to follow.

In the first place, I notice that the title of the Church is different in the Letter from that which is used in the Prayers. In the first paragraph of the Letter the author claims to follow the teachers "of the Catholic and *Apostolic* Church," and again to represent the faith "of the holy Catholic and *Apostolic* Church." Now the titles of the Church in the Liturgies (like the wording of the doxologies) are by no means accidental, but follow distinct lines, and are, generally, within certain limits, very uniform. In Sarapion's Liturgy the word "Apostolic" nowhere occurs. The title of the Church is three times "Catholic" (once with "living"). Once (in the Didaché passage) it is "holy" alone. Once in no. 23 we have the fuller title, which is so markedly Egyptian, "thy holy and only Catholic Church." (See index, s.v. ἐκκλησία.) On the other hand, the title "Catholic and Apostolic" is by no means unknown to other Liturgies. It is found in the Syrian Liturgy (*Ap. Const.* p. 10, and with "holy," *St. James*, p. 45). It is found combined, with other titles, in various types of the Egyptian rite. It is not found, however, in the Nestorian or Persian, which has simply "holy Catholic Church," pp. 263, 264, 275. The usage, therefore, of the dogmatic Letter may be Egyptian, though it is strictly identical only with that of the *Apostolic Constitutions.*

Then again the doxology with which the Letter ends is not Trinitarian in any way, as Sarapion's doxologies are, and it has a rather rhetorical form. Instead of ending, "to all the ages of the ages," it concludes—"To the unseen wise God honour and might, greatness, magnificence both now and ever, yea was and is and shall be to generations of generations and to the ageless incorruptible ages of the ages. Amen."

The style of the Letter is in fact both inflated and obscure, while in thought it is simple enough. Part is so obscure or so corrupt—possibly through the loss of sentences or even pages—that I find it impossible to give a reasonable version of it, even after conjectural emendation.[1]

[1] I refer to chap. 3, p. 22, lines 14—30. I should suggest

But the style of the Prayers, though Eastern
rather than Western, is not inflated, and the
meaning is always clear.

If then these arguments are valid, we need lay
no stress upon the supposed insufficiency of the
teaching about the holy Spirit in the dogmatic
Letter as affecting Sarapion. It is of course to be
noticed that the author of that Letter interprets
"the bosom of the Father," in St. John i. 18, as the
sum of the divine Attributes, and as equivalent to
"the holy Spirit." It is that "in which are all
virtues and powers and energies of the Father,"
just as in the heart of man are all his powers and
virtues which are enumerated at some length.
This teaching does not seem heretical, but it is
hardly sufficient.

I incline, therefore, to attribute the dogmatic

---

reading, " εἰ οὖν ἐπὶ μήκει (W. ἐπιμήκει) τοῖς κατὰ δέησιν καὶ
βραχυτάτοις ταῦτα καὶ λέγεται (W. λέγετε), γίνεται πόσως
κ.τ.λ."

I imagine, though it is rather a stretch of exegetical
imagination, that the author means—" If then such things
can be said about (the) extent (of the power of) those who
have a precarious and very short existence, how immense
is the ocean of the Father's greatness?" But I cannot
make out the lines that follow later (21—24), even reading
πῶς for ὅπως. There seems to be something lost after μόνον
δὲ αὐτὸν ἔδωκεν : and the construction in a later sentence of
τῶν διαφερόντων τῶν δεξιῶν τῆς δικαιοσύνης, which are apparently divided between ἀρχαὶ δυνάμεις and ἐξουσίαι, is very
harsh and artificial. The mention of Θεότητες or " divini-
ties" amongst angelic powers is also strange.

Letter to some other author than Sarapion. But it would seem likely that the author belonged to the Egyptian Church, since all the other authors whose writings are collected in the MS. (Athanasius, Euthalius, Sarapion) are of that country.

§ 4. *The Collection of Prayers, their general contents, style, and character.   Unity of their style. Evidence of Egyptian origin.*

The thirty Prayers may be divided into six groups or sections:—I. (1—6) *Eucharistic Anaphora*, containing the second half of the Liturgy, usually called the Anaphora, and including blessing of oil and water, apparently as food for the sick. II. (7—11) *Baptismal Prayers.* III. (12—14) *Ordination Prayers ;* including only those for Deacons, Presbyters, and a Bishop. There is no mention of Subdeacons or Readers, but they are prayed for together with Interpreters in no. 25. IV. (15—17) *Blessing of Oils*, including Oil before Baptism, Chrism for what we call Confirmation, and Oil for the sick, bread or water. V. (18) *Commendation of the Dead.* VI. (19—30) *Proanaphoral Prayers* to be said before no. 1. There is a rubric at the end of no. 30. " All these Prayers are performed before the Offertory Prayer," if we may so render πρὸ τῆς εὐχῆς τοῦ προσφόρου—a striking phrase in which the offertory of the people and the oblation of the Eucharistic gifts seem to be combined. This is the title given in the collection itself to no. 1, which is called " Offertory Prayer of Bishop Sarapion." These six groups together form what we may call a Pontifical, or Ἀρχιερατικόν, *i.e.* a Bishop's Prayer-book. They contain nothing for the people to say, except the Tersanctus, which would no doubt be said by all together, and nothing for the Deacons, and they have in two places the pronoun " I," which is very uncommon in such documents (see nos. 3 and 19). They involve at least a second celebrant or concelebrants besides the Bishop, since the Bishop, who of course was celebrant, is prayed for as " this Bishop," in no. 25.

There is no reference to Lections or Psalms,[1] and nothing distinctly implying the Hand-washing and the Kiss of Peace, though there is a Prayer, no. 24, *Prayer concerning the Church*, which might not unfitly have been said with reference to both ritual acts. The Lord's Prayer does not occur, but Mr. Brightman conjectures that the heading of no. 2 may refer to it as having been said. Further there is no mention of incense, and no reference to the Intercession

---

[1] The Creed was not introduced into the Liturgy till a considerably later date.

of Saints, nor any invocation of them, direct or indirect. The nearest approach to such an attitude is found in no. 29—"May this people be blessed by the blessing of (the) Spirit, by the blessing of heaven, by the blessing of prophets and apostles." (*Cp.* 26, " Number us together with thy holy prophets and Apostles " ; and 27, " Let them be joined in symmetry with the heavenly ones, let them be numbered together with the angels ; let them become entirely elect and holy.")

Speaking generally, the Prayers are extremely pious and scriptural, and free from anything superstitious. The practice of invocation, however, especially over things to be given to the sick, *e. g.* in no. 17, might perhaps lend too much countenance to the use of charms. While the circle of ideas is not very wide, there is a great naturalness and vivacity in the expression. The graces aimed at are principally purity, cleanness, health, life, truth, and knowledge. " Life," in various forms of expression, is a remarkable note of the collection : *e. g.* in no. 1 the bread and cup, *before consecration* are called a " living sacrifice." In no. 1 again we read " make one living Catholic Church." So in 6, " Let their bodies be living bodies," and 14, " make also this Bishop a living Bishop." I am not aware of any

author in whose works similar language is found,
but it seems quite appropriate to a man living
amidst the formalism and monotonous routine
of existence in the Delta, and desiring to see it
elevated.   There is no mention of persecution,
and the life mirrored in the Prayers seems to be
even and quiet.   We have already spoken in § 2
of the absence of direct reference to idolatry.
There is little recognition of special difficulty ;
and the recollection of the world outside the
Church, in prayers for rulers and for the con-
version of the heathen, is very slight.   In 27
we read, "We pray for all rulers : may they
have a peaceable life."   I have already referred
to this prayer in § 2 as suiting a date A.D. 350—
356 for the collection.   No. 20, the *Prayer on
rising up from sermon*, is more interesting than
usual :—

"Send holy Spirit [on this people] and let the Lord
Jesus visit them, let Him speak in the understandings
of all, and predispose their hearts to faith : may
He Himself draw their souls to Thee, O God of compassions : create a people even in this City, create a
genuine flock through thy only begotten Jesus Christ in
holy Spirit ; through whom to thee (is) the glory and the
strength both now and to all the ages of the ages.   Amen."

All the thirty Prayers, except two, end with
this formula : "to all the ages of the ages.
Amen" ; and the two exceptions, viz. (18) the
Burial Prayer, and (25) *For a Bishop and the*

Church, end similarly, " to the ages of the ages. Amen." All, that is to say, end with the doxology, generally in the Trinitarian form of which the quotation just made from no. 20 is an example. (See above, end of § 2.)

The phraseology of the Prayers as well as their general structure gives them a very marked character, and connects them together by a bond of remarkable unity of style. An enumeration of the most strikingly recurrent words and phrases will establish this.

The word μονογενής, " only-begotten," occurs in every Prayer, and in several more frequently, *e.g.* 1 (5), 5 (2), 7 (2), 10 (2), 12 (3), 13 (3), etc. In all it occurs fifty times. It is of course used with intention, and it is seen to be a mark of date when compared with the use of παῖς, in the Didaché and the *Canons of Hippolytus.* Next in frequency is καθαρός, "clean," and its derivatives, which occur twenty-four times, viz. 3, 6, 11, 12, 13, 15, 19 (3), 21, 24 (7), 25 (3), 27 (2), 29 (2).

Other frequently recurring words are φιλάνθρωπος,[1] which I have rendered " lover of men " or " loving," and " loving-kindness," or φιλανθρωπία, which occur thirteen times, viz. 1, 3, 4, 6, 7, 8,

[1] An epithet of divine wisdom in Wisdom i. 6, vii. 23. It is frequent in the Egyptian Liturgies.

10, 15, 22, 23, 26, 27 (2) ; ζωὴ, ζῶν, "life," "living,"
which occur also twelve times, and as we have
seen in very remarkable phrases, viz. 1 (4), 6, 14,
16, 20, 24 (2), 25, 28, 29; and the titles of God
ἀγένητος, "uncreated," nine times, viz. 1 (3), 5, 7,
13, 26, 27, 28 ; "God of truth" (cp. Ps. xxxi. 6),
ten times, viz. 1 (3), 2, 6, 8, 9, 11, 15, 27, and "God
of compassions" (cp. 2 Cor. i. 3), six times, viz.
2, 3, 20, 26, 27, 30. Other characteristic titles
are φιλόπτωχος, "lover of the poor" (found in
Athanasius) in 1, and φιλόψυχος,[1] "lover of souls,"
15, 26 ; εὐεργέτης, "benefactor," 7, 10, 26, 27 ; and
δημιουργός, "artificer," 7, 11, 19, 20, 23.

Certain almost technical terms are ἐπικαλεῖσθαι,
"to invoke," occurring seven times, viz. 1, 15, 16,
17, (2), 23, 25 ; ἐνέργεια, "energy," ἐνεργεῖν, "to
work in," 7, 15 (2), 16, 17 ; ἑρμηνεύειν, "to interpret"
and its compounds, and ἑρμηνευτής, "interpreter,"
1 (2), 19, 25 ; ἐπιδημία and ἐπιδημεῖν, of the
"advent" "coming" or "on-dwelling" of the
Logos, 1 (2), 7, 13 ; προκοπή, "advancement,"
1 (3), 3, 25, in the last two cases with βελτίωσις,
"improvement" ; γνήσιος, "genuine" or "own,"
9, 14, 20, 24, 27 ; τιμᾶν, "to honour," in the
peculiar sense of "to adorn," 10, 22 (2) ; and
συγχωρεῖν, "to give indulgence" or "to forgive"

---

[1] This also is from the book of Wisdom, which appears
to have had special influence in Egypt.

4, 24, 26. The words " Satan " or " Satanic " occur in 15, 16, 17, 21.[1]

These words are so evenly distributed over the whole collection, that every Prayer, however short, contains three and generally more instances, except the " Commendation of the dead" (no. 18), which has only one, and the last of all, which has two. To be perfectly accurate, we ought also to notice that no. 5 only has ἀγένητος and two instances of μονογενής, not three separate words of our list. Every prayer ends with *Amen*.

This similarity of phraseology is supported by a great similarity of structure, which however is not so easy to indicate except by asking the reader to notice the opening as well as the closing words of the different Prayers, particularly the doxology.

It may be well to notice some of the indications which support what we know of the Egyptian origin of the collection. Others will be evident to those who compare the general

[1] It will be noticed by those familiar with the literature of the *Apostolic Constitutions*, that there is very little similarity in this list to the peculiar phraseology of that author, for which see Brightman, pp. xxiv—xxviii. Almost the only words common to the two writers (among those quoted by Brightman) are δημιουργός, κοινωνεῖν, συγχωρεῖν. Sarapion uses ἀγένητος "uncreated"; the author or editor of *Ap. Const.* uses ἀγέννητος "unbegotten."

structure of the services with the Egyptian
rites.

The occurrence of the title to no. 19, " First
Prayer of the Lord's Day," is closely parallel to
" the first Prayer of the morning," in *Lit. of
Coptic Jacobites*, p. 147, a peculiar feature of the
Egyptian rite. The epithet " only " in the title
of the Church, in no. 23, is a remarkable characteristic of the Liturgies of this country,
occurring in *St. Mark*, pp. 121, 126, and *Coptic
Jacobites*, 150, 160, 161, 165, 166, 168, and I
believe nowhere else. The reference to " Solitaries" in so early a document, in no. 25, is in
the same line. The Prayer for " Interpreters" is
undoubtedly suitable, especially in connection
with the traditional position of St. Mark, though
the evidence for the character of the office had
hitherto been Syrian. The remarkably simple
Benediction of Presbyters (13, see below, pp.
50—52) is only paralleled, as far as I know, by
that still used by the Abyssinian Jacobites. In
the Liturgy we have a piece of the Preface
almost verbally identical with a passage of the
Liturgy of St. Mark. Some words from the
Didaché shortly after, comparing the gathering
of the Church into one body to the gathering of
grain scattered upon the mountains into a single
loaf, are found (in a grace before meat) nearly

in the same form in a book "on Virginity,"
ascribed, though with little probability, to St.
Athanasius (*Did.* ix. 4=*de virginitate*, § 13).
There is nothing in the Prayers that seems
against an Egyptian origin.   The Prayers for
rain (23), which at first sight might seem out of
place, are found also in *St. Mark*, pp. 119, 127,
and *Coptic Jacobites*, pp. 159 and 168, where they
are also connected with Prayers for the rising of
the river.   The latter, however, were not needed
in that part of the Delta where Thmuis lay,
which has a sufficient supply of river-water.
Rain may be expected in Lower Egypt in the
early months of the year, though not generally
in great amount.   According to Baedeker's
Handbook, p. lxvii, 1895—"The whole of the base
of the Delta lies within the region of the winter
rains, which, from January to April, are blown
inland by the prevailing sea-breezes to a distance
of 30—50 English miles."   The mean rainfall
at Alexandria, for a period of fourteen years,
is stated by the same author to have been eight
inches.   Just before I visited Cairo, in January
1898, there had been very heavy rain, which
stood in some places nearly a foot deep in the
streets.   On the other hand, in Upper Egypt rain
is of very rare occurrence.   There was, however,
a great rain-storm at Thebes in October 1898.

§ 5. *The Eucharistic Liturgy. The Pro-anaphora.*

It is not difficult to reconstruct the general course of the Eucharistic Liturgy, as regards the celebrant's part, by simply taking Prayers 19—30 and prefixing them to 1—6. Thus we get the Pro-anaphoral portion in its right position before the Anaphora. Why the two parts were so disjoined opens up an interesting question in the history of Liturgies which cannot be treated here at length, but three things may be concluded—(1) that the Anaphora was first set down separately as the more important part; (2) that next in importance were considered the Prayers for other sacramental acts; (3) that the Pro-anaphoral Prayers were less fixed, especially in their order. It is in regard to these that we find less certainty of order in this collection and less regularity of parallelism with other Egyptian rites. It is noticeable also that the Liturgy of St. Mark is defective in its earlier portions, as if they were not considered so important, and that of the "Ethiopic Church ordinances" consists only of an Anaphora.[1]

---

[1] We have noticed also in § 2, p. 17, that the doxology in the *Apostolic Constitutions* is differently worded in the Pro-anaphora and the Anaphora, as if they were taken from different editions in separate books.

The Pro-anaphoral portion here given may be divided into three sub-sections, viz. (1) Prayers of the Catechumens (19—21) ; (2) Prayers of the Faithful (22—27) ; (3) Benedictions (28—30). It may be concluded that the Prayers in each section are for the most part relatively in proper order, though several prayers in sub-section 2 are puzzling. The Benedictions obviously form a separate collection. We may presume that they were at first pronounced *ad libitum*, and only gradually became formal. They would also be a separate sub-section, as being reserved only for the Bishop, whereas the rest might (on occasion) be said by one who was not a Bishop. The three Benedictions in this collection must obviously be introduced at three various points of the service.

It may be convenient for the reader to have before him the short fourth-century account of the Liturgy which is given in the Canons of the Council of Laodicea in Phrygia—a Council unfortunately of uncertain date, but probably somewhat later rather than earlier than Sarapion's Liturgy. It is fixed to the period between A.D. 343—381, and these Canons were evidently intended to introduce something like ritual uniformity, though at first in a comparatively small area.

c

"Canon 16.—That on the Sabbath, Gospels should be read together with other Scriptures.

"Canon 17.—That Psalms should not be said in a series, but that a lection should be read between each Psalm and the next.

"Canon 18.—That the same service of Prayers should always be said both at Nones and Vespers.

"Canon 19.—That the Prayer of catechumens should be gone through (ἐπιτελεῖσθαι) first by itself after the Sermons of the Bishops, and after the exit of the Catechumens the Prayer of the Penitents should come, and when they have come forward for Benediction (προσελθόντων ὑπὸ χεῖρα) and departed, on that (οὕτως) should come the Prayers of the Faithful, three in number : one, and that the first, said silently, and the second and third recited with a loud voice, and on that the Peace should be given : and after the Presbyters have given the Peace to the Bishops, then the laymen shall give the Peace, and on that the holy oblation should be celebrated (ἐπιτελεῖσθαι): and that only sacerdotal persons (τοῖς ἱερατικοῖς) should be allowed to enter the sanctuary and to communicate (there)."

The following is an attempt to show the sequence of the Prayers and their relation to the rites, mainly by the assistance of parallel

drawn from the other Egyptian Liturgies, viz.—
St. Mark (M), the *Liturgy of the Coptic Jacobites
(Coptic or C)*, and the *Anaphora of the Ethiopic
Church Ordinances (E.C.O.)*, and the *Liturgy of
the Abyssinian Jacobites (Abyss. or A)*. Reference
also is made here and there to the *Liturgy of
the Apostolic Constitutions*. All these are edited
by Mr. Brightman, and numerals refer to his
pages. References to the *Canons of Hippolytus
(C.H.)* are to the sections of Achelis' edition
(1891). The titles in *italics* are those of the
original Prayers. Titles in SMALL CAPITALS are
chiefly those of Mr. Brightman's divisions.
Details in [square brackets] are gathered from
other Liturgies, but are more or less conjectural.

Before reading the table, the student may be
reminded that it is uncertain how far the rules
laid down by the Council of Laodicea were
acted upon or expressed widespread and accepted principles. Ritual uniformity is not
easily secured, and Phrygia of course had no
control over Egypt. Certainly in this Liturgy we
have no reference to the dismissal of Penitents,
nor can I find parallels to the 1st and 3rd of the
"three (great) Prayers" of the Faithful, which
are contained in *M, C,* and *A,* after which the
"Peace" was given. The word Peace nowhere
occurs in Sarapion ; and I am inclined to bring

the kiss, following some symbolic ablution
into connection with no. 24, and therefore to
put it earlier than the one Prayer (25) which
clearly answers to the central Prayer of the
"three Prayers" of the Faithful in *M, C, A.*
Nos. 26 (*Prayer of bending the knee*) and 27
(*Prayer on behalf of the people*) are peculiar, the
first in its title, and the second in its contents,
as it falls really into two parts. I believe,
however, that both these Prayers are in their
right place relatively to the others, and capable
of reasonable explanation as preludes to the
offerings of the people. It may be remarked
that Εὐχή is generally used of a Prayer of the
celebrant (see Brightman, Glossary, *s. v.*).

Tabular View of the Liturgy of Sarapion.

PRO-ANAPHORA.

[Opening Collect.]

19. *First Prayer of the Lord's Day: cp.* " First
Prayer of the morning," *Coptic,* 147, and parallel
Abyss. 202. *Cp. St. Mark,* 117, and the Western
collect.

PRAYERS OF THE CATECHUMENS.

[The Lections: Epistle of St. Paul, Catholic
Epistle, Acts, Gospel; Sermon.]

20. *Prayer after rising up from the sermon:*

cp. " O long-suffering," *C.* 157, and " O far from Anger," *A.* 220.

21. *Prayer on behalf of the Catechumens : cp.* petitions in the " Remember, O Lord," *C.* 157, 30, *A.* 221, 26.

28. *Benediction of Catechumens.*

[Dismissal of Catechumens.]

[N.B. 7—11. When Baptism took place, the newly baptized would remain for Communion. It would seem likely that Baptism and Confirmation were, at any rate, occasionally intercalated here.]

PRAYERS OF THE FAITHFUL.

[Deacon's Litany or Ectene for the people : *St. Mark* 119, *C.* 159.]

29. *Benediction of the people.*

22. *Prayer for those who are sick: cp. M.* 119, *C.* 157, *A.* 220.

30. *Benediction of the sick.*

23. *Prayer for fruitfulness : cp. M.* 119, *C.* 157, *A.* 220.

24. *Prayer concerning the Church : cp. C.* 162–3, *A.* 226–7.

[This Prayer is markedly one for cleanness. It implies the ministry of those who take part in it, *i. e.* the Faithful, who are about to offer and join in the hymns and prayers. It mentions men, women, and children. I believe it to be connected with the Hand-washing, or ablutions of some kind, followed by the Kiss. Ablutions, especially in Egypt, may have been practised by the people as well as the clergy.]

[The Hand-washing and the Peace ?][1]

25. *Prayer on behalf of a Bishop and the Church.*

[This answers clearly to the second of the " three (great) Prayers " (cp. *Can. Laod.* 19) of *M.* 121, *C.* 160–1, *A.* 223, which are the first for peace, the second for the Bishop and clergy, etc., the third for the safe meeting of the congregations ; but the first and third topics are not found in Sarapion.]

[Then follow the Confessions of the People.]

26. *Prayer of bending the knee,*[2] and

---

[1] St. Cyril, *Cat. Myst.* v. 2, 3, describes the Hand-washing and the Kiss at some length. The kiss after Baptism is frequently also referred to, *e.g. C. H.* xix. 139, 141.

[2] No. 26 is difficult, because it differs from other prayers connected with γονυκλισία (*Ap. Const.* viii. 9, p. 9, and *C.* 158), and because kneeling was generally forbidden on Sundays and Festivals (*Can. Nic.* 20). But the action is natural in a confession of sin, and it would perhaps be pedantic to suppose that the prohibition of kneeling was absolute in the early Church, or universally accepted. Such confessions are referred to in the Didaché 14, and *Canons of Hippolytus,* 9. If 26 was said kneeling, or with alternate kneeling and standing (as *C.* 158), so no doubt was 27.

27. *Prayer on behalf of (the) people*, which are evidently closely connected, and are, if in right order, confessions of sin preparatory to or coincident with the Offertory. The first is the celebrant's intercession for them, the second consists of two parts :—

A. Prayer in the name of the people, and implying their concurrence, as far as, "To thee we dedicate ourselves ; receive us, O God of truth."

B. "Fixed diptych" on behalf of those who make offerings, beginning, "Receive this people" (see Mr. Brightman's Glossary, *s. v.* "Diptych"). The nearest parallels in Egyptian Liturgies to 26 and 27 are the "Prayer of Penitence," etc., which follow the Lord's Prayer and the Inclination, in *A*. 235 foll.

[N.B. 12, 13, 14. After these confessions would be intercalated the Ordination Benedictions whenever an ordination took place (as in *Can. Hipp.* 9 foll.). The newly-created Bishop would bless the offerings and take part in the celebration (*ib.* 20). A single Benediction or χειροθεσία was apparently all the ceremony required after proper election and acceptance, etc.]

THE OFFERTORY.

§ 6. *The Eucharistic Liturgy* (*continued*). *Tabular view of the Anaphora.* It will be convenient to give the table at once, and to add the notes afterwards.

ANAPHORA.

THE THANKSGIVING.

[The Lord be with all :

℞ And with thy spirit.

Lift up your hearts :

℞ We lift them up unto the Lord.

Let us give thanks unto the Lord :

℞ It is meet and right.]

1. *Offertory Prayer of Bishop Sarapion*, consisting of the following parts—

A. Preface ending with the Sanctus : *M.* 125 . . . 132 ; *C.* 164 . . . 176 ; *A.* 228–231. There is no Preface in *E.C.O.*

B. Oblation and Recital of the Institution, beginning with the second " Full is the heaven " : *M.* 132 ; *C.* 176 ; *A.* 232. Cp. *E.C.O.* 189 foll.

C. Invocation of the Logos : *cp.* S. Iren. iv. 18, 5, and v. 2, 3, S. Hieron. *in Sophon.* iii., Migne, *P. L.* xxv. 1377.

[The Invocation of the holy Spirit is in *M.* 133 ; *C.* 178 ; *E.C.O.* 190 ; *A.* 233.]

D. Intercession for the living : *M.* 126 ; *C.* 165 ; *A.* 228 [before Oblation and Invocation].

E. Intercession for the departed : *M.* 128 ; *C.* 169 ; *A.* 229, 236.

Recitation of the Diptychs : *M.* 129 ; *C.* 169; *A.* 236.

F. Prayer for those who have offered : *M.* 129.

G. Lord's Prayer (?).

THE MANUAL ACTS AND COMMUNION.

2. After the [Lord's ?] Prayer (comes) the Fraction, and in the Fraction a Prayer.

[The Fraction here referred to is evidently a μελισμός for distribution, as *M.* 138. In *C.* 177 and *A.* 238 the Fraction comes after the recital of the Institution, as with ourselves.]

[The Inclination.]

3. After giving the Fraction to the Clerics, Benediction of the People: M. 136–7 ; *C.* 183 ; *E.C.O.* 191. It is not found in *A.*

[Post Communion Prayer.]

4. After the distribution of (i. e. *to*) *the People* (*is this*) *Prayer:* cp. *M.* 141 ; *C.* 186; *E.C.O.* 192 ; *A.* 240.

OFFERING OF OILS AND WATERS.

5. Prayer concerning the oils and waters that are offered. [The usual place for such a Prayer is after the recital of the Institution, and such a Prayer is actually found in *E.C.O.* 190 after the Invocation.   Mr. Brightman, in his Glossary, *s. v.* "Oils, oblation of," draws attention to the fact that other oils were consecrated at this point, such as for Baptism, Confirmation, and Unction of the Sick, as they still are on Maundy Thursday.   The close connection, however, of 5 and 6 shows that in this Liturgy such consecration took place for the use of the people generally after Communion.   The other oils (see § 9 and 15, 16, 17) were probably consecrated *pro re nata*, as was the case in the service described in *C.H.* xix. 116, 117.]

6. *Benediction after the blessing of oils and waters.*   This prayer refers to the Eucharist as having been celebrated and the Communion received, and is evidently the final Benediction : *cp.* "the Inclination," *M.* 142 ; *C.* 187 ; *E.C.O.* 192 ; *A.* 243.

DISMISSAL OF THE FAITHFUL.

———

Having made an attempt to settle the order and general significance of the Prayers of the Anaphora, I will make some observations on its most striking points.

The *first* is the verbal identity of certain sentences in the Preface with the Liturgy known as that of St. Mark—a feature quite natural in an Egyptian document.

The *second* is its emphatic use of the word "likeness" in reference to the relation of the bread and cup to the body and blood of Christ, and its attachment of the thought of Sacrifice to the bread and cup *before* consecration. This is what we should expect from what we read in Tertullian, Justin and Irenaeus, and it helps us to understand their language.

Thirdly, we remark the use of the Gospel records of the Institution as giving a narrative justifying the offering of the bread and cup, the types or "likeness" of the body and blood, not as part of the actual Prayer of Consecration which comes later. This agrees with St. Paul's reference to the history of the Passion in connection with the Eucharist (1 Cor. xi. 26), where he treats it as a Haggâdah, like that referred to in Exodus xii. 26 foll. and xiii. 8 foll. as giving the reason for the Passover.

Fourthly, we note that our Lord's words are quoted in a short and somewhat unusual form : "Take ye, eat, this is my body, which is being broken for you for remission of sins," and—in reference to the cup "after supper"—"Take ye, drink, this is the new covenant, which is my blood, which is being poured out for you for

remission of sins" (" sins " is a slightly different
word, in the second place). The first sentence
is closely akin to other Egyptian forms : the
second is, I think, not found exactly elsewhere.
There is no mention of our Lord's act of
blessing, and no decided reference to the words,
" Do this in remembrance of me," though the
context would lead one to expect it. Such a
reference is omitted also in the Byzantine St.
Chrysostom.

Fifthly, between the offering of the bread and
that of the cup is inserted a Prayer for the union
of the Church, drawn from the Didaché, immediately following our Lord's words in regard to
the bread, as follows—

" Wherefore we also making the likeness [1] of His death
have offered the bread, and beseech thee by this sacrifice,
O God of truth, be reconciled to us all and have mercy :
and as this bread was scattered upon the mountains and
gathered together became one, so gather together thy
holy Church from every nation and every country and
every city and village and house, and make one living
catholic Church. We have also offered the cup, the
likeness of the blood, because the Lord Jesus Christ
taking a cup after supper said to his disciples, etc."

The Sacrifice of the Church, therefore, according to this prayer, is that of the bread and
wine which are chosen as the *likeness* of the body

[1] This is the nearest reference to the " Do this in remembrance of me."

and blood of Christ. It is as types of His offering that they are offered by the Church : not simply as first-fruits of the creatures. There is no further offering of them after consecration, but a thankful and reverent use in communion.

Lastly, the consecration, which comes almost at the end, is clearly performed by the Invocation, and that not of the Holy Spirit, but of the Logos, the prayer being addressed to the "God of truth," as follows—

"O God of truth, let thy holy Word come (ἐπιδημησάτω) upon this bread, that the bread may become body of the Word, and upon this cup, that the cup may become blood of the truth ; and cause all that communicate to receive medicine of life for healing of every sickness and for strengthening of all progress and virtue, not for condemnation, O God of truth, and not for censure and reproach ; for we call upon thee the uncreated through the only-begotten in holy Spirit."

Then follow Prayers for the people and for the faithful departed—the latter referring to the recitation of their names and asking for their "sanctification," and that they may have "a place and mansion in God's kingdom." Lastly is a prayer that the thanksgiving or eucharist of the people may be received, and they who have offered "offerings" (πρόσφορα) and "thanksgivings" may be blessed. These "offerings" probably include the bread and wine for communion and gifts for a common meal or Agapé or for the sick. There is no mention of the Lord's Prayer unless perhaps in the heading of 2.

The form of Invocation asking for the coming of the Logos upon the bread and cup has certain analogues in Gnostic Eucharistic prayers,[1] and is traceable in several ecclesiastical writers. In St. Irenaeus " receiving the Word, of God in v. 2, 3, answers to "receiving the Invocation of God," iv. 18, 5. The language of Clement and Origen on the relation of the Eucharist to the Word (Clement, *paed.* i. 6 and ii. 2 ; Origen *in Matt.* series 85, etc.) naturally prepared the way for such an Invocation in Egypt. St. Athanasius writes : " Whenever the great prayers and the holy supplications have been sent up, the Word comes on the bread and cup and they become his body " (*fragmenta alia 7 ad baptizandos* : *P.G.* xxvi. 1325). We may also compare a Mozarabic *Postpridie* Collect for the 3rd Sunday in Advent (*P.L.* lxxxv. 129).

The language of St. Jerome is important as bearing on the use of ἐπιδημία in the Liturgy, and as showing that the " coming of the Lord " was in question. In his commentary on Zephaniah he bids the priests, *i. e.* Bishops, not to be

---

[1] I have given references to them in my book on *The Holy Communion*, ed. 2, p. 142. They are direct Invocations of a divine power to " come."

indignant at the strong language he employs, but to make use of it ; and incidentally he describes their offices as "qui dant baptismum, *et ad Eucharistiam Domini precantur adventum,* faciunt oleum chrismatis, manus imponunt," etc. (*in Sophon.* iii., Migne, *P. L.* xxv. 1377). The "Prayer for the advent of the Lord at the Eucharist"[1] can hardly be anything but a reference to such an Invocation as we have here,—"adventus" being the regular equivalent of ἐπιδημία.[2]

It appears, then, that in various parts of Christendom, up to the fourth century, a Prayer for the advent of the Second Person of the

---

[1] It is not necessary to discuss other passages in which the coming of the Logos may possibly be intended, such as 1 Tim. iv. 5. ("Every creature of God is good and nothing is to be rejected, if it be received with thanksgiving : for it is sanctified through the word of God and prayer" ; *cp.* below, no. 17, *Prayer for oil of the sick, or for bread, or for water,* and Justin *Apol.* 66) In the latter passage indeed δι' εὐχῆς Λόγου τοῦ παρ' αὐτοῦ it may be that we ought to understand the Lord's Prayer and translate "by the word of prayer which is from Him" (*i.e.* from Christ) ; or "by the prayer of the Logos who is from God," *i.e.* by the prayer of blessing used by our Lord, the words of which are lost, but the virtue of which remains to sanctify the Bread and Cup.

[2] See Suicer, s.v., who quotes it frequently in the form εἰς or πρὸς ἀνθρώπους. The religious use of ἐπιδημία is illustrated by the passages quoted in L. Preller's *Griech. Mythologie,* pp. 197-8 (1872), about the ἀποδημία and ἐπιδημία of Apollo. Ἐπιδημία is also used of the solemn entrance of a Governor into his Province.

Trinity upon the Eucharistic oblation took the place afterwards usually assigned to the Invocation of the Third Person. How the change took place, and why it has left so little mark on history, we have as yet insufficient means of judging; but it may be certainly concluded that it was connected with the development of the doctrine of the holy Spirit which was forced upon the Church by Macedonian error.

A learned theologian of our own diocese (Canon Powell) suggests to me that in the early conceptions of the doctrine of the Trinity, "the Logos is the centre of the divine action, and His action carries with it or includes that of the holy Spirit." This is no doubt true; but in these earlier Liturgies, as far as we can gather, the Word was named and not the holy Spirit; while in later ones the Spirit was named and not the Word. This is the point to be noticed. It is rather remarkable that in the first of our reformed Liturgies (that of 1549), "holy Spirit and word" are united, while in the various forms of the Scottish Liturgy it is "Word and holy Spirit," and so in the American Prayerbook. I take it that in 1549 something of this early patristic language was known, but "word" was interpreted of the gospel narrative as in the Western Church generally.

§ 7. *The Baptismal Prayers*, 7—11.

This collection of five Prayers does not offer
so much that is strikingly new. The first prayer
called *Sanctification of Waters* of course implies
a stage in Liturgical development above that of
the earliest, in which it would seem that no consecration prayer was needed for the water.
The Teaching of the Apostles and Justin Martyr
say nothing of the consecration of the water or
font. The Canons of Hippolytus, § 112, order
Baptism "in pure running sea-water prepared,
sacred"—collected apparently in some vessel
or *piscina*, into and out of which it runs.
The words are, "prope fluctuantem aquam
maris puram, paratam, sacram." The latter
words imply some prayer of consecration; and
this was also the rule in St. Cyprian's time
(*Ep.* 70, 1). Apparently, as with ourselves,
the hallowing was part of the actual service as
occasion arose. The parallel to the consecration
of the bread and cup, by Invocation upon the
waters of the presence of the Word, is very
close; but the prayer is also, "fill them with
holy Spirit." The service proper clearly began
with a renunciation of evil spirits (no. 9), the
false gods especially of heathenism, the prayer
connected with it being, "that he may no longer
minister to those that are worse, but may

D

worship in the God of truth." After the renunciation doubtless came the anointing with
the ἄλειμμα, elsewhere called "oil of exorcism"
or "oil of Catechumens," consecrated according
to the form given in no. 15. This prayer is
assigned particularly to Sarapion, Bishop of
Thmuis, and it is perhaps right to conjecture
that this oil of exorcism was not regarded as
very important in Egypt before his time. It
was, however, in use one hundred and fifty
years earlier at Rome, if we may judge by
the *C. H.* xix. 116 foll. (see note on the Prayer).
There is also apparently an allusion to the recitation of the Creed, but it is rather obscure. The
separation of Confirmation from Baptism, in
theory at any rate if not in practice, is evident
from the fact that Confirmation is only referred
to in the Blessing of Chrism, no. 16. The
change in the rite as regards the Ministry of
the Bishop is discussed in § 9.

§ 8. *The Ordination Prayers*, 12—14.

Next to the Eucharistic Anaphora, the most
important prayer in the collection is that of the
Benediction of Presbyters (13). Its simplicity
reminds us of the often-quoted form in use
among the Abyssinian Jacobites with which it
ought to be compared.[1]

[1] That form may be given here from Ludolf, *Comment.
in Hist. Æth.* p. 328, 1691 :—

It entirely disposes of what is apparently the contention of Pope Leo XIII., that the "order of Priesthood or its grace and power, which is chiefly the power of consecrating and of offering the true body and blood of the Lord," must be expressed in the "form" to make it valid. (See the Bull *Apostolicae Curae* (1896), § 7.)

The thoughts are largely those of the English Ordination Service.   The office of a steward and ambassador, and the ministry of reconciliation, are all touched upon ; but the "order of priesthood" is not mentioned, and there is no reference to any sacramental acts, except that of reconciliation.   In no. 25, the occasional prayer for a Bishop and his "fellow-presbyters" is equally simple.   For the latter it is, "cleanse

---

"My God, Father of our Lord and Saviour Jesus Christ, regard this thy servant, and bestow on him the Spirit of grace and the counsel of holiness, that he may be able to rule thy people in integrity of heart ; as thou regardedst thy chosen people, and commandedst Moses to elect elders, whom thou filledst with the same Spirit with which thou endowedst thy servant and thy attendant Moses.   And now, my Lord, give to this thy servant the grace which never fails, continuing to us the grace of thy Spirit, and our sufficient portion ; filling our hearts with thy religion that we may adore thee in sincerity.   Through, etc."   See also Bp. Bel's Letters on the subject in E. E. Estcourt, *The Question of Anglican Ordinations Discussed:* Appendices xxxiii.-xxxv., Lond. 1873.   The subject is touched on in the Appendix to *Answer of the Archbishops of England to the Apostolic Letter of Leo XIII.*, Notes 3 and 4.   Longmans : 1897.

them, give them wisdom, give them also knowledge and right doctrine ; make them to be
ambassadors of thy holy doctrine rightly and
unblameably." In the case of the deacons there
is a reference, in this occasional prayer, to their
share in the ministry of " the holy body and the
holy blood." But there is no definite reference
to any sacrament in any of the three Ordination
" forms," and we have seen that, strange as it
may seem, the name " Presbyter " is entirely
absent from no. 13. It may of course be *inferred*
distantly from the reference to the "chosen
ones," *i. e.* the seventy Elders chosen by Moses.
I need not say that in our earliest English type
of ordination service the title of " Priest " was
not only inferred, but expressed, and that four
times—(1) in the act of presentation, (2) in the
Bishop's reply to the Archdeacon, (3) in the
collect, which then preceded the examination,
(4) and in the examination itself. The word
" Ministers," in the " Thanksgiving " after the
Veni Creator, is also clearly used of the second
order of the ministry. This document, then,
comes in, and that in a most striking manner, to
confirm the argument of our Archbishops in
their reply to the Pope's Bull.

It may be remarked that the word χειροθεσία
or " laying-on-of-hands " is widely used in these

Prayers (3, 6, 28, 29, 30) as well as in the Ordination Prayers, in the sense of Benediction, no
doubt with outstretched hands. It may be that
actual touch was not considered essential; and
this almost seems to be implied in the often-
quoted phrase of St. Augustine *De bapt. contra.
Don.* iii. 16: "Quid est aliud (manus impositio)
nisi oratio super hominem?" *i. e.* "What is
laying on of hands except prayer over a man?"
Cp. *Conc. Tolet.* iv. 13, where we read of "im-
positiones manuum" being composed, like hymns
and prayers.

Doubtless actual touch was originally intended
in all Benedictions, as we should gather from the
ὑπὸ χεῖρα προσελθεῖν of the Laodicene Canon (§ 5
above), and the "ad manum episcopi accedere,"
so frequent in the accounts of the Liturgy of
Jerusalem furnished by the Spanish pilgrim now
known as Etheria or Egeria. But as numbers
increased, actual touch probably dropped in
many cases, and extension of hands was substi-
tuted. So it was in the Roman Church in regard
to Confirmation, and in the Ordination of Presbyters at the time of saying what is clearly the
old "form" of ordination, the long prayer which
can be traced back to the earliest Sacramentaries.[1]

[1] This change was pointed out in the *Answer of the
Archbishops of England to the Apostolic Letter of Leo
XIII.*, chaps. x. and xix., 1897.

The absence of Benedictions of minor orders, Subdeacons, Readers, and Interpreters, shows that they had not yet risen to much importance, though prayed for in no. 25 (see note there). In their case earlier documents expressly *forbid* them to be ordained with imposition of hands. See *Can. Hipp.* vii. 48 for Readers, and *Egyptian Ch. Ord.* (Lagarde), 36, for Subdeacons. *Cp.* Achelis, *Can. Hipp.* p. 70 and 140, and Wobbermin, p. 34. The text of *Ap. Const.* viii. 20—22 in fact contradicts the documents on which it is based.

§ 9. *Blessing of Oils,* 15—17. *Development of Confirmation.*

We have already spoken (§ 7) of Sarapion's Benediction of the Oil to be used before Baptism. It would seem that it and the Chrism for use after Baptism were consecrated at first when they were needed, as is implied by the words βαπτιζόμενοι, χρίονται: and this is explicitly stated in *C. H.* xix. 116, 117, and *Eth. C. O.* 46.

It is disappointing to find no more distinct directions as to the use of the Chrism in the Prayer-book before us, as they might have explained to us how the difference grew up between East and West in regard to the ministry of Bishops in Confirmation. All that is implied is, that it was used to anoint, and that in the

process of anointing, the sign of the Cross
(ἐκτύπωμα, " impress," also σφραγίς, " seal ") was
made on the person—no doubt on the forehead,
and possibly elsewhere. It is the more disappointing as the *Canons of Hippolytus* have
recently thrown great light on the Roman
usage, and have explained some points in
Western controversy, and the development generally of the rite.   I quote it here as the earliest
Confirmation Office that has come down to us.

According to those Canons both the Oil of
exorcism and the Chrism were consecrated,
before the service, by the Bishop.   They were
applied, however, by Presbyters.   The second of
them crossed the forehead and breast with the
Chrism, and anointed the whole body, head, and
face, saying, " I anoint thee in the name of the
Father, Son, and holy Spirit."   Then the Bishop
lays hands on all who had been baptized, saying:

" We bless thee, Almighty Lord God, for that thou hast
made these [*thy servants*] worthy to be born again, and
over whom thou pourest out thy holy Spirit, in order that
they may now be united to the body of the Church, never
to be separated by alien works.   Rather give also to them,
to whom thou hast already given remission of sins, the
earnest (ἀρραβῶνα) of thy kingdom through our Lord Jesus
Christ, through whom to thee with him and the holy
Spirit (be) glory to the ages of the ages.   Amen."

Then he marks their foreheads with the sign of
love and kisses them, saying—

" The Lord be with you : "

and the baptized reply—

" And with thy Spirit."

Thus he does for each of those who have been baptized.   Now they pray with all the people who kiss them, rejoicing with them with exultation.   *Canons of Hippolytus*, 116, 117, 134—140.

As regards the usage in Egypt in the fourth century, I think we may argue from the *silence* of Sarapion, and from the present practice of the Greek Church, that the Bishop's part in Confirmation, as far as the Chrism was concerned, consisted in blessing it and in superintending its application, made, as in *C. H.*, by a Presbyter probably with a very short formula, perhaps like that at present in use, " The seal of the gift of the holy Spirit."   As Baptism and the anointing with Chrism took place in early ages before the Offertory, those who had first received the double rite would have imposition of hands from the Bishop in the Liturgy with the rest of the Faithful ; and this was (I imagine) thought to follow the Apostolic example sufficiently.   After a time, when the Bishop was not always present at Baptism and the Eucharist, the Chrism was blessed separately, and his personal part in the rite was forgotten, at least in the Eastern Church.

In the West the right of the Presbyter to
apply the Chrism was gradually restricted, and
the Bishop became the "ordinary minister"
throughout. It has, however, been always, I
think, the tradition that the duty of Confirmation might under certain circumstances be
delegated to Presbyters. Amongst us it may
be said that the "sealing" with the sign of the
Cross is regularly delegated to them in the
Baptismal Office.

The Oil for the Sick (no. 17) was also apparently consecrated immediately before use,
as we may judge by the words, "these thy
servants."

§ 10. *Commendation of the Dead* (no. 18).

This Prayer partakes of the nature both of a
commendation of one who is dying and of a
prayer over one who is dead. It would seem to
have been said in the house, before the funeral.
This I judge from the rubric ἐκκομιζομένου (being
carried forth), and the word ἔξοδος (going forth)
in the prayer. The earliest descriptions in
detail of burial services are in *Apost. Const.* vi.
30 and viii. 41. In the first of these the word
ἔξοδοι is used for funeral processions. The
second contains both the Deacon's and the
Bishop's part, and is evidently for use at the
altar. It mentions the Hebrew patriarchs by

name, but otherwise bears little similarity to our prayer. The silence of Sarapion's liturgy rather suggests that in his church burial took place the same evening, and that there was no Eucharistic celebration connected with it. A rather full description of burial rites is to be found in Pseudo-Dionysius, *De Eccles. Hierarchia*, vii. 347—360, ed. Paris, 1644.

It will be noticed that this prayer, which has considerable beauty, differs somewhat in style from the rest.

§ 11. *Miscellaneous Remarks.*

I have endeavoured to make the version of the following Prayers as accurate as possible, even at the risk of a certain want of smoothness. It is more important for the reader to know whether the English word before him represents a Greek word occurring elsewhere in the collection, than to have a comfortably-sounding and familiar phrase. The list of words in § 4 will give an idea of the most frequently-recurring and remarkable phrases, and the English which represents them. I have kept "clean" for καθαρός throughout, and "power" for δύναμις, except that I have sometimes felt obliged to render it " Hosts " where it occurs in the plural. But the English *Te Deum* and *Benedicite omnia opera* have partially familiarized us with

"Powers" in the same sense. "Provider" stands for χορηγός, "sanctify" = ἁγιάζειν, and "sanctification," ἁγιασμός, except where otherwise stated.

I have suggested two or three rather obvious emendations, which are referred to in the notes to chapters 14, 17, 23. But, generally speaking, Dr. Wobbermin has done his part very well.

Those who have seen the tentative Introduction which I published in the *Salisbury Diocesan Gazette* for April 1899, and the version which was brought out with it in a limited issue by Messrs. Brown & Co. in that city in May, will find that this Introduction is almost rewritten, and of much greater length, and the version and notes revised to a considerable extent.

JOHN SARUM.

West Lulworth,
St. Barnabas' Day (11 *June*), 1899.

Revised 15 *Nov.* 1909.

In revising this second edition I have had the advantage of using Canon Brightman's text and notes in the *Journal of Theological Studies* for Oct. 1899 and Jan. 1900 and some other notes published since. I could have wished to add more, but it has been thought best to leave the greater part as it stood. J. S.

THE PRAYERS

I. (1—6) EUCHARISTIC ANAPHORA.

1. *Offertory Prayer of Bishop Sarapion.*

[A. PREFACE.]

IT is meet and right to praise, to hymn, to glorify thee the uncreated Father of the only-begotten Jesus Christ. We praise thee, O uncreated God, who art unsearchable, ineffable, incomprehensible by any created substance. We praise thee who art known of thy Son (St. Matt. xi. 27; St. John x. 14, 15), the only-begotten, who through him art spoken of and interpreted and made known to created nature. We praise thee who knowest the Son and revealest to the Saints the glories that are about him : who art known of thy begotten Word, and art brought to the sight and interpreted to the understanding of the Saints. We praise thee, O unseen Father, provider of immortality. Thou art the fount of life, the fount of light, the fount of all grace and all truth, O lover of men, O lover of the poor, who reconcilest thyself to all, and drawest all to thyself through the advent (ἐπιδημία) of thy beloved Son. We beseech thee make us living men. Give us a spirit of light, that "we may know thee the true [God] and him whom thou didst send, (even) Jesus Christ" (St. John xvii. 3). Give us holy Spirit, that we may be able to tell forth and to enuntiate thy unspeakable mysteries. May the Lord Jesus speak in us and holy Spirit, and hymn thee through us.

* For thou art " far above all rule and authority and power and dominion, and every name that is named, not only in this world but also in that which is to come" (Eph. i. 21). Beside thee stand thousand thousands and myriad myriads of angels (Dan. vii. 10; Heb. xii. 22), arch-angels, thrones, dominions, principalities, powers (*lit.* rules, authorities) : by thee stand the two most honourable six-winged seraphim, with two wings covering the face, and with two the feet, and with two flying and crying holy (ἀγιάζοντα, *cp.* Isa. vi. 2, 3), with whom receive also our cry of " holy " (ἀγιασμόν) as we say : Holy, holy, holy, Lord of Sabaoth, full is the heaven and the earth of thy glory.

* See the note on next page.

[B. OBLATION AND RECITAL OF THE INSTITUTION.]

Full is the heaven, full also is the earth of thy excellent glory.* Lord of Hosts (*lit.* powers), fill also this sacrifice with thy power and thy participation (μεταλήψεως): for to thee have we offered this living[1] sacrifice (Rom. xii. 1), this bloodless oblation (*cp.* Eph. v. 2). To thee we have offered this bread the likeness (ὁμοίωμα) of the body of the only-begotten. This bread is the likeness of the holy body, because the Lord Jesus Christ in the night in which he was betrayed took bread and broke and gave to his diciples saying, "Take ye and eat, this is my body which is being broken for you for remission of sins" (cp. *Lit. of St. Mark, etc.*). Wherefore we also making the likeness of the death have offered the bread, and beseech thee through this sacrifice, be reconciled to all of us and be merciful, O God of truth: and as this † bread had been scattered on the top of the mountains and gathered together came to be one, so also

* There is much similarity in the passage between these asterisks to the parallel passage in the Liturgy of St. Mark, but the differences are also striking.

[1] *Cp.* the phrase of the Nestorian Liturgy which speaks of the Body and Blood of Christ as being on the altar before consecration (Brightman, p. 267).

gather thy holy Church out of † every nation and
every country and every city and village and
house and make one living catholic church. We
have offered also the cup, the likeness of the
blood, because the Lord Jesus Christ, taking a
cup after supper (Luc. xxii. 20; 1 Cor. xi. 25), said
to his own disciples, " Take ye, drink, this is the
new covenant, which (ὅ) is my blood, which is
being shed for you for remission of sins (ἁμαρτη-
μάτων)." Wherefore we have also offered the
cup, presenting a likeness of the blood.

[C. INVOCATION OF THE LOGOS.]

O God of truth, let thy holy Word come
upon this bread (ἐπιδημησάτω . . . ἐπὶ τ.ἄ.τ.) that
the bread may become body of the Word,
and upon this cup that the cup may become
blood of the Truth ; and make all who communicate to receive a medicine of life for the
healing of every sickness and for the strengthening of all advancement and virtue, not for condemnation, O God of truth, and not for censure
and reproach. For we have invoked thee, the
uncreated, through the only-begotten in holy
Spirit.

† . . .† This thought is borrowed from the *Teaching of
the Apostles*, ch. ix. 4 : *cp.* [S. Ath.] *de Virginit.* 13.

[D. INTERCESSION FOR THE LIVING.]

Let this people receive mercy, let it be counted worthy of advancement, let angels be sent forth as companions to the people for bringing to naught of the evil one and for establishment of the Church.

[E. INTERCESSION FOR THE DEPARTED.]

We intercede also on behalf of all who have been laid to rest, whose memorial we are making.

After the recitation (ὑποβολήν [1]) *of the names:* Sanctify these souls: for thou knowest all. Sanctify all (souls) laid to rest in the Lord. And number them with all thy holy powers and give to them a place and a mansion in thy kingdom.

[F. PRAYER FOR THOSE WHO HAVE OFFERED.]

Receive also the thanksgiving (eucharist) of the people, and bless those who have offered the offerings (τὰ πρόσφορα) and the thanksgivings, and grant health and soundness and cheerfulness and all advancement of soul and body to this whole people through the only-begotten Jesus Christ in holy Spirit; as it was and is and shall be to generations of generations and to all the ages of the ages.   Amen.

---

[1] In Socrates *H. E.* v. 22, p. 296, ὑποβολεῖς are mentioned with 'Readers': see Valesius' note and my index, p. 104.

[G.   THE LORD'S PRAYER?]
[THE MANUAL ACTS AND COMMUNION.]

2. *After the [Lord's?] prayer (comes) the fraction,
and in the fraction a prayer.*

Count us worthy of this communion also, O
God of truth, and make our bodies to contain
purity (χωρῆσαι ἀγνείαν) and our souls prudence
and knowledge.   And make us wise, O God of
compassions, by the participation of the body
and the blood, because through thy only-begotten to thee (is) the glory and the strength
in holy Spirit, now and to all the ages of the
ages.   Amen.

[THE INCLINATION.]

3. *After giving the fraction (i.e. the broken bread)
to the clerics, imposition of hands (i. e. Benediction)
of the people.*

I stretch out the hand upon this people and
pray that the hand of the truth may be stretched
out and blessing given to this people on account
of thy loving kindness (φιλανθρωπίαν), O God of
compassions, and the mysteries that are present.
May a hand of piety and power and sound
discipline (σωφρονισμοῦ) and cleanness and all
holiness bless this people, and continually pre-
serve it to advancement and improvement

E

through thy only-begotten Jesus Christ in holy
Spirit both now and to all (the) ages of the ages.
Amen.

[POST COMMUNION PRAYER.]

4. *After the distribution of (i. e. to) the people (is
this) prayer.*

We thank thee, Master, that thou hast called
those who have erred, and hast taken to thy self
those who have sinned, and hast set aside the
threat that was against us, giving indulgence by
thy loving kindness, and wiping it away by
repentance, and casting it off by the knowledge
that regards thyself (τῇ πρὸς σὲ γνώσει ἀποβαλών).
We give thanks to thee, that thou hast given
us communion of (the) body and blood. Bless
us, bless this people, make us to have a part
with the body and the blood through thy only-
begotten Son, through whom to thee (is) the
glory and the strength in holy Spirit both now
and ever and to all the ages of the ages. Amen.

[OFFERING OF OILS AND WATERS.]

5. *Prayer concerning the oils and waters that
are offered.* [1]

We bless through the name of thy only-

[1] A parallel prayer to this may be found in *Apost. Const.*
viii. 28, and in *Anapora of E.C.O.* p. 190. *Cp.* no. 17.

begotten Jesus Christ these creatures, we name
the name of him who suffered, who was crucified, and rose again, and who sitteth on the
right hand of the uncreated, upon this water
and upon this [oil].   Grant healing power upon
these creatures that every fever and every evil
spirit (δαιμόνιον) and every sickness may depart
through the drinking and the anointing, and
that the partaking of these creatures may be a
healing medicine, and a medicine of soundness,
in the name of thy only-begotten Jesus Christ,
through whom to thee (is) the glory and the
strength in holy Spirit to all the ages of the
ages.   Amen.

[FINAL BENEDICTION.]

*6. Laying on of hands (i e. Benediction) after the
blessing of the water and the oil.*

O loving (φιλάνθρωπε) God of truth, let the
communion of the body and the blood go along
with (συμπαραβαινέτω) [1] this people.   Let their
bodies be living bodies, and their souls be clean
souls.   Grant this blessing to be a keeping of
their communion, and a security to the Eucharist
that has been celebrated : and make blessed all
of them in common and make (them) elect

[1] This is a rare use of the word.   We might almost
translate "continue with."

through thy only-begotten Jesus Christ in holy Spirit both now and to all the ages of the ages. Amen.

[DISMISSAL OF THE FAITHFUL.]

II. (7—11) BAPTISMAL PRAYERS.

7. *Sanctification* (ἁγιασμός) *of Waters.*

King and Lord of all things and Artificer of the world, who gavest salvation freely to all created nature by the descent of thy only-begotten Jesus Christ, thou who didst redeem the creation (πλάσμα) that thou didst create by the coming (ἐπιδημίας) of thy ineffable Word : see now from heaven and look upon these waters and fill them with holy Spirit. Let thine ineffable Word come to be in them and transform (μεταποιησάτω) their energy and cause (κατασκευ-ασάτω) them to be generative (as) being filled with thy grace, in order that the mystery which is now being celebrated (ἐπιτελούμενον) may not be found in vain in those that are being regenerated, but may fill all those that descend (into them) and are baptized (herein) with the divine grace. O loving benefactor spare thy own handiwork (τοῦ σοῦ ποιήματος), save the creature that has been the toil of thy right hand. Form all that are being regenerated (after) thy divine

and ineffable form, in order that having been
formed and regenerated they may be able to
be saved and counted worthy of thy kingdom.
And as thy only-begotten Word coming down
upon the waters of the Jordan[1] rendered
(ἀπέδειξεν) them holy, so now also may he
descend on these and make them holy and
spiritual, to the end that those who are being
baptized may be no longer flesh and blood, but
spiritual and able to worship thee the uncreated
father through Jesus Christ in holy Spirit,
through whom to thee (is) the glory and the
strength both now and to all the ages of the
ages.   Amen.

8. *Prayer on behalf of those being baptized.*

We beseech thee, O God of truth, on behalf
of this thy servant and pray that thou wouldst
count him worthy of the divine mystery and
of thy ineffable regeneration.   For to thee, O
loving (God), is he now offered ; to thee we
devote (ἀνατίθεμεν) him : grant him to communi-

[1] Note that there is no mention of the Ark or of the
Red Sea or of the Pauline thought of death and burial
with Christ in Baptism.   The latter is emphasized in the
short parallel prayer *Apost. Const.* vi. 43.   Baptism into
Christ's death is a note of the theology of that writer
(see Brightman, p. xxvi. 43, and xxviii. 6).   (*Cp.*, however,
no. 15.)

cate in this divine regeneration, to the end that
he may no longer be led by any bad and evil
one, but worship (λατρεύειν) thee continually
and observe thy ordinances as thy only-begotten Word doth guide him : for through him to
thee (is) the glory and the strength in the holy
Spirit both now and to all the ages of the ages.
Amen.

9. *After the renunciation* (ἀποταγήν) [1]—*a prayer.*

O Lord all-sovereign seal the adhesion
(συγκατάθεσιν) of this thy servant which has now
been made to thee, and continually keep his
character and his manner (of life) unchangeable,
that he may no longer minister to those that are
worse, but may worship (λατρεύῃ) in the God of
truth, and serve thee the maker of all things, to
the end that he may be rendered perfect and
thine own (σοί γνήσιον) through thy only-begot-

[1] The earliest form of this is given in *C. H.* xix. 119,
"I renounce thee, O Satan, with all thy company
(*pompa*)"—a remarkable phrase, from which comes, I
presume, our baptismal phrase about "the pomps and
vanities of this wicked world." After this the candidate
was anointed with the "oil of exorcism" (cp. no. 15 and
note), and made a short confession of faith : "I believe
and bow myself in thy presence, and in that of all thy
company (*pompa*), O Father, and Son, and Holy Spirit."
From other authorities we find that it was customary for
the Catechumen to say, with hands outstretched towards
the East, "I adhere (συντάσσομαι) to Christ."

ten Jesus Christ, through whom to thee (is) the glory and the strength in holy Spirit both now and to all the ages of the ages. Amen.

10. *After the acceptance* (ἀνάληψιν)[1]—*a prayer.*

O loving benefactor, saviour of all those who have turned to thee for succour, be gracious (ἵλεως) to this thy servant. Guide him to the regeneration with thy right hand: let thy only-begotten Word guide him to the washing (λουτρόν): let his regeneration be honoured, let it not be empty of thy grace: let thy holy Word accompany him, let thy holy Spirit be with him scaring away and driving off every temptation, because through thy only-begotten Jesus Christ (is) the glory and the strength both now and to all the ages of the ages. Amen.

11. *After* (*he*) *has been baptized and has come up—a prayer.*

O God, the God of truth, the Artificer of all,

[1] This word may either mean "acceptance," "acknowledgement," *i. e.* acceptance of the candidate by God, as a child is acknowledged by its father, or by the Bishop who has heard him say the Creed; or, as Dr. Wobbermin suggests (p. 36), "restoration," "recovery," *i. e.* restoration of the person to his lost relation to God. In either case it is the word here answering to the συνταγή or "adhesion" (σύνταξις, Cyril, *Cat. Myst.* i. 8) to Christ. This was generally made by the recitation of a creed, to which, however, there is no distinct reference here. Brightman reads ἄλειψιν, anointing, and connects it with no. 15.

the Lord of all the creation, bless this thy
servant with thy blessing : render (δεῖξον) him
clean in the regeneration, make him to have
fellowship with thy angelic powers, that he may
be named no longer flesh but spiritual, by partaking of thy divine and profitable gift. May
he be preserved up to the end to thee the Maker
of the world (τῶν ὅλων) through thy only-begotten
Jesus Christ, through whom (is) to thee the glory
and the strength in holy Spirit both now and to
all the ages of the ages. Amen.

III. (12—14) ORDINATION PRAYERS.

12. *Laying on of hands of the making* (κατα-
στάσεως) *of Deacons.*

Father of the only-begotten who didst send
thy Son and didst ordain the things (πράγματα)
on the earth, and hast given rules to the Church
and orders (τάξεις) for the profit and salvation
of the flocks, who didst choose out Bishops,
Presbyters, and Deacons for the Ministry of thy
catholic Church, who didst choose through thine
only-begotten the seven Deacons, and didst
freely give to them holy Spirit, make also this
man a Deacon of thy catholic Church, and
give in him a spirit of knowledge and discern-
ment, that he may be able cleanly and unblame-

ably to do service in this ministry in the midst of the holy people, through thy only-begotten Jesus Christ, through whom to thee (is) the glory and the strength in holy Spirit both now and to all the ages of the ages.   Amen.

13. *Laying on of hands of the making of Presbyters.*[1]

We stretch forth the hand, O Lord God of the heavens, Father of thy only-begotten, upon this man, and beseech thee that the Spirit of truth may dwell (*or* settle) upon him.   Give him the grace of prudence and knowledge and a good heart.   Let a divine Spirit come to be in him that he may be able to be a steward of thy people and an ambassador of thy divine oracles, and to reconcile thy people to thee the uncreated God, who didst give of the spirit of Moses upon the chosen ones, even holy Spirit.   Give a portion of holy Spirit also to this man, from the Spirit of thy only-begotten, for the grace of wisdom and knowledge and right faith, that he may be able to serve thee in a clean conscience (1 Tim. iii. 9), through thy only-begotten Jesus Christ, through whom to thee (is) the glory and the strength in holy Spirit both now and for all the ages of the ages.   Amen.

[1] See *Int.* § 8, p. 50 foll., on this important prayer.

14. *Laying on of hands of the making of a Bishop.*

Thou who didst send the Lord Jesus for the gain of all the world (οἰκουμένης), thou who didst through him choose the apostles, thou who generation by generation dost ordain holy Bishops, O God of truth, make this Bishop also a living Bishop, holy [1] of the succession of the holy apostles, and give to him grace and divine Spirit, that thou didst freely give to all thy own (γνησίοις) servants and prophets and patriarchs : make him to be worthy to shepherd thy flock and let him still continue unblameably and inoffensively in the Bishopric through thy only-begotten Jesus Christ, through whom to thee (is) the glory and the strength in holy Spirit both now and to all the ages of the ages. Amen.

IV. (15—17) BLESSING OF OILS.

15. *Prayers (corr. προσευχαί) of Sarapion, Bishop of Thmuis: a prayer (εὐχή) in regard to (εἰς) the anointing oil (ἄλειμμα) of those who are being baptized.*[2]

---

[1] ἅγιον.—Perhaps we should read ἄξιον, " worthy."

[2] See *Int.* § 7, p. 50, § 9, p. 55, and cp. *Can. Hipp.* xix. § 116, 118 foll. ; St. Cyril of Jerusalem, *Cat. Myst.* ii. 3 ; and *Apost. Const.* iii. 15, and esp. vii. 42, where a prayer somewhat similar to this is described. This unction is not

Master, lover of men and lover of souls
(Wisd. xi. 26), compassionate and pitiful, O God
of truth, we invoke thee following out and obey-
ing the promises of thine only begotten who
has said, "whosesoever sins ye forgive, they are
forgiven them" (St. John xx. 23) : and we anoint
with this anointing oil those who in purpose
approach this divine regeneration, beseeching
(thee) that (ὥστε) our Lord Jesus Christ may
work in them healing and strength-making
power, and by this anointing oil may reveal
(himself) and heal away from their soul, body,
spirit, every mark of sin and lawlessness or
satanic fault, and by his own proper grace may
afford them remission, that dying (ἀπογενόμενοι)
to sin they shall live to righteousness (1 Pet. ii.
24), and being re-created through this anointing,
and being cleansed through the washing, and
being renewed in the spirit (Eph. iv. 23), they
shall be able henceforth to have victory over all
the opposing energies and deceits of this world

---

mentioned by Justin, Tertullian, or Cyprian, and seems to
have been unknown to Augustine. (See *D. Chr. Ant.* s. v.
Baptism, § 47, by W. B. Marriott.) But it appears to have
been customary in Rome at an earlier date, being described
at length in *C. H.* l. c. No form of Blessing is, however,
given there. It seems probable that these three oils were
blessed when they were needed, as the prayers imply the
presence of the persons concerned.

that assail them, and thus to be bound up and
united with the flock of our Lord and Saviour
Jesus Christ, because through him to thee (is)
the glory and the strength in holy Spirit to all
the ages of the ages. Amen.

16. *Prayer in regard to the Chrism with which
those who have been baptized are being anointed*
(χρίονται).

God of Hosts (*lit.* powers), the helper of every
soul that turns to thee and that cometh under
the mighty hand of thy only-begotten, we invoke
thee to work in this chrism a divine and heavenly
energy [1] through the divine and unseen powers
of our Lord and Saviour Jesus Christ, in order
that they who have been baptized, and who are
being anointed with it with the impress (ἐκτύπωμα)
of the sign of the saving cross of the only-
begotten, by which cross Satan and every
opposing power was routed and triumphed over,
they also, as being regenerated and renewed
through the washing of regeneration (παλιν-
γενεσίας, Titus iii. 5), may become partakers of
the gift of the holy Spirit, and being made

---

[1] *Cp.* the parallel prayer *Apost. Const.* vii. 44, which,
however, is much shorter as being said over each who
receives the chrism, and has otherwise very little
similarity. For the development of this rite see above,
Int. § 9, pp. 54—57.

secure by this seal (1 Cor. xv. 53), may continue steadfast and unmoveable, unhurt and inviolate, free from harsh treatment and intrigue, in the franchise (ἐμπολιτευόμενοι) of the faith and full knowledge of the truth, awaiting to the end the heavenly hopes of life and eternal promises of our Lord and Saviour Jesus Christ, through whom to thee (is) the glory and the strength both now and to all the ages of the ages. Amen.

17. *Prayer in regard to oil of the sick or for bread or for water.*[1]

We invoke thee who hast all authority and power, the Saviour of all men, father of our Lord and Saviour Jesus Christ, and pray thee to send healing power of the only-begotten from heaven upon this oil, that it may become to those who are being anointed (with it), or are partaking of these thy creatures, for a throwing off of every

[1] This Benediction, like the two that precede it, seems to have been used *pro re nata*, and not on any special day like Maundy Thursday or at the Eucharist, as no. 5 clearly was. This is implied by the words " These thy servants " towards the close. Its connection with bread and water for the use of the sick is consistent with the application of the oil by the sick persons themselves, as was sometimes done, especially in the Western Church. In the East, however, the presence and ministry of Presbyters was more insisted on in connection with St. James v. 13—15.

sickness and every infirmity (Matt. iv. 23), for a charm (ἀλεξιφάρμακον) against every demon, for a separation (ἐκχωρισμόν [1]) of every unclean spirit, for an expulsion (ἀφορισμόν) of every evil spirit, for a driving out of all fever and ague (ῥίγους) and every infirmity, for good grace and remission of sins, for a medicine of life and salvation, for health and soundness of soul, body, spirit, for perfect strengthening (ῥῶσιν). O Master, let every Satanic energy, every demon, every device of the adversary, every plague, every scourge (μάστιξ), every pain, every labour or stroke (ῥάπισμα) or shaking (ἐντίναγμα) [2] or evil shadowing (σκίασμα), fear thy holy name which we have now invoked and the name of the only-begotten ; and let them depart from the inward [and] the outward parts of these thy servants, that his name may be glorified who for us was crucified and rose again, who took up (ἀναλαβόντος) our sicknesses and our infirmities, (even) Jesus Christ (cp. Matt. viii. 17), and who is coming to judge quick and dead. Because through him to thee (is) the glory and the strength in holy Spirit both now and to all the ages of the ages. Amen.

[1] This word is not in the dictionaries.
[2] Wobbermin mistakenly prints this ἐντείναγμα, though ἐντίναγμα is the MS. reading. Cp. Sirach, xxii. 13 v. l. Isa. xxviii. 2, and xxxii. 2 ed. Aquila.

V. COMMENDATION OF THE DEAD.

18. *Prayer for one who is dead and is to be carried forth* (ἐκκομιζομένου).[1]

God, who hast authority of life and death (Wisd. xvi. 13), God of the spirits and Master of all flesh (*cp.* Num. xvi. 22), God who killest and makest alive, who bringest down to the gates of Hades and bringest up (1 Sam. ii. 6), who createst the spirit of man within him and takest to thyself (παραλαμβάνων) the souls of the saints and givest rest, who alterest and changest and transformest thy creatures, as is right and expedient, being thyself alone incorruptible, unalterable and eternal, we beseech thee for the repose (κοιμήσεως) and rest of this thy servant or this thine handmaiden : give rest to his soul, his spirit, in green places (ἐν τόποις χλόης, *cp.* LXX. Ps. xxii. 2), in chambers (ταμείοις) of rest with Abraham and Isaac and Jacob and all thy Saints : and raise up his body in the day which thou hast ordained, according to thy promises which cannot lie (Titus i. 2), that thou mayest render to it also the heritage of which it is worthy in thy holy pastures. Remember not

[1] See above, *Int.* § 10. This prayer was apparently said, like our "commendatory prayer," in the chamber of death.

his transgressions and sins : and cause his going forth (ἔξοδον) to be peaceable and blessed.
Heal the griefs of those that pertain to him (τῶν
διαφερόντων) with the spirit of consolation, and
grant unto us all a good end through thy only-
begotten Jesus Christ, through whom to thee
(is) the glory and the strength in holy Spirit to
the ages of the ages.   Amen.

VI. (19—30) PRO-ANAPHORAL PRAYERS.
[OPENING COLLECT.]

19. *First Prayer of the Lord's Day* (κυριακῆς).[1]

We beseech thee the Father of the only-
begotten, the Lord of the universe (τοῦ παντός),
the artificer of the creatures, the maker of things
that have been made ; clean hands do we stretch
out, and our thoughts do we unfold (ἀναπετάννυμεν)
to thee, O Lord.   We pray thee, have compassion, spare, benefit, improve, multiply (us) in
virtue and faith and knowledge.   Visit us (Ps.
cxv. 4), O Lord ; to thee we display (ἀναπέμπομεν)
our own weaknesses.   Be propitious and have
pity on us all in common.   Have pity, benefit
this people.   Make it gentle (ἐπιεικῆ) and sober-
minded and clean ; and send angelic powers, in

---

[1] This rubric is one which specially connects this
collection with Egypt : *cp.* "the first prayer of the morning" in the *Lit. of the Coptic Jacobites*, Brightman, p. 147.

order that all this thy people may be holy and
reverend (σεμνός). I beseech thee send holy
Spirit into our mind and give us grace to learn
the divine scriptures from (the) holy Spirit, and
to interpret,[1] cleanly and worthily, that all the
lay-people (λαοί) present may be helped, through
thy only-begotten Jesus Christ in holy Spirit,
through whom to thee (is) the glory and the
strength both now and to all the ages of the
ages. Amen.

[PRAYERS OF THE CATECHUMENS.]

20. *After rising up from* (ἀπο) *the sermon—a
prayer.*[2]

God, the Saviour, God of the Universe, the
Lord and artificer of the world (τῶν ὅλων), the
begetter of the only-begotten, who hast begotten
the living and true expression (of thy self, ἀληθινὸν
χαρακτῆρα, *cp.* Heb. i. 3), who didst send him for
the help of the race of men, who through him
didst call and make men thy own possession,
we pray thee on behalf of this people. Send

---

[1] This may be simply a prayer for capacity to explain
the Scriptures, or it may refer to the special gift of
interpretation from one language to another : see below,
Prayer 25 note.

[2] The Sermon is generally and properly after the Gospel
and just before the dismissal of penitents and others who
cannot communicate.

holy Spirit (on them), and let the Lord Jesus
visit them, let him speak in the understandings
of all, and predispose their hearts to faith ; may
he himself draw their souls to thee, O God of
compassions. Create a people even in this City,
create a genuine flock through thy only-begotten
Jesus Christ in holy Spirit, through whom to
thee (is) the glory and the strength both now
and to all the ages of the ages. Amen.

21. *Prayer on behalf of the Catechumens.*[1]

Helper and Lord of all, deliverer (ἐλευθερωτά)
of those who have been delivered, protector
(προστάτα) of the rescued, the hope of those who
have come under thy mighty hand : thou art
he who hast put down lawlessness, who through
thy only-begotten has brought Satan to nought
and hast loosed his devices and released those
who were bound by him : we thank thee on
behalf the Catechumens, because thou hast
called them through the only-begotten, and
freely gavest to them thy knowledge. May
they be confirmed in (this) knowledge, that they
may know thee the only true God and him
whom thou didst send (even) Jesus Christ (St.
John xvii. 3). May they be continually guarded
in what they have learnt and in clean wisdom

---

[1] This was no doubt followed by no. 28.

(καθαρᾷ φρονήσει), and may they advance to become worthy of the washing of regeneration (Titus iii. 5), and of the holy mysteries, through the only-begotten Jesus Christ in holy Spirit, through whom to thee (is) the glory and the strength both now and to all the ages of the ages. Amen.

[PRAYERS OF THE FAITHFUL, BEGINNING WITH A LITANY FOLLOWED BY THE BENEDICTION NO. 29.]

22. *Prayer for those who are sick.*[1]

We beseech thee the overlooker and Lord and fashioner of the body and maker of the soul, thee who didst fit together man, thee who art the steward and governor of the whole race of men, thee who art reconciled and made gentle because of thine own love of men : be propitious Master : assist and heal all that are sick. Rebuke the sicknesses : raise up those that are lying down : give glory to thy holy name and to that of thy only-begotten Jesus Christ, through whom to thee (is) the glory and the strength in holy Spirit, both now and to all the ages of the ages. Amen.

[1] This no doubt was followed by 30.

23. *Prayer for fruitfulness.*

Artificer of heaven and earth, thou who hast crowned the heaven through the choir of the stars, and made it brilliant through the Luminaries, who hast honoured[1] earth with its fruits for the profit of men, thou † who hast freely given to the race that has been created by thyself,† from above to enjoy the ray and the light of the Luminaries, and from below to be nourished from off the fruits of the earth. We pray thee grant (us) the rains most full and most fertilizing.[2] Cause the earth also to bear fruit and to produce in great abundance on account of thy loving-kindness and goodness. Remember those who invoke thee: honour thy holy and only[3] catholic Church and hear our supplications and prayers, and bless all the earth, through thy only-begotten Jesus Christ, through whom to thee (is) the glory and the strength in holy Spirit both now and to all the ages of the ages. Amen.

[1] Honoured = adorned; cp. Horace, *Od.* xvii. 16, etc.

† . . . † The words χρησάμενος τῷ γένει τῷ ὑπὸ σοῦ πεπαλαιωμένῳ do not make sense. The true reading may be conjectured to be χαρισάμενος . . . πεπλασμένῳ.

[2] There are prayers for rain and for the rising of the Nile in the *Liturgy of St. Mark* (pp. 119 and 127, Brightman) and the *Liturgy of the Coptic Jacobites* (*ib.* pp. 159, 168). The latter prayer was not needed at Thmuis. On the occurrence of rain in Egypt see § 4, p. 31.

[3] An Egyptian title: see *Int.* § 4, p. 30.

24. *Prayer concerning the Church.*[1]

O Lord God of the Ages, O God of reasonable spirits, O God of clean souls and of all who invoke thee in simplicity (γνησίως) and cleanness, thou who in heaven art manifested and brought to the knowledge of clean spirits, who on earth art hymned and dwellest in the catholic Church, who art ministered to by holy angels and clean souls, who also madest out of the heavens a living chorus to (the) glory and praise of the truth, grant that this Church may be a living and clean Church, grant it to have divine powers and clean angels as ministers, that in cleanness it may be able to hymn thee. We beseech thee on behalf of all persons (ἀνθρώπων) of this Church ; be reconciled to all, give indulgence to all, give remission of sins to all. Grant them no longer to sin in anything, but become a wall to them and bring to nought every temptation. Have mercy on men, and women, and children : and show thyself in all ; and let the knowledge of thyself be written in their hearts, through thy only-begotten Jesus Christ, through whom to thee (is) the glory and

[1] This prayer, in which the importance of cleanness is seven times emphasized, seems to be naturally connected with some form of ablution, followed by the kiss of peace. See *Int.* § 5, pp. 35–6, 37–8.

the strength in holy Spirit both now and to all
the ages of the ages. Amen.

[THE HAND-WASHING AND THE PEACE ?]

---

25. *Prayer on behalf of a Bishop and the Church.*[1]

We invoke thee the Saviour and Lord, the
God of all flesh and the Lord of every spirit,
thou that art blessed and the provider of every
blessing, sanctify this Bishop[2] and keep him
outside every temptation, and give to him wisdom and knowledge. Lead him rightly in thy
rules of discipline (ἐπιστήμαις). We beseech thee
also for the Fellow-presbyters, sanctify them,
give them wisdom and knowledge and right
doctrine: cause them to be ambassadors of
thy holy doctrine rightly and unblameably.
Sanctify also the Deacons, that they may be
clean in heart and body and be able to minister
(λειτουργῆσαι) in a clean conscience and to give
attendance (παραστῆναι) to the holy body and
the holy blood. We beseech thee also on
behalf of the Subdeacons and Readers and

[1] This clearly answers to the second of the " Three
(great) prayers" in the Egyptian Liturgies. The first for
peace and the third for the safety of the congregations
do not occur here. See *Int.* § 5, p. 38.

[2] This prayer, then, might be said by an assistant Bishop
or Presbyter. The Bishop and his Presbyters were
properly always con-celebrants.

Interpreters.[1] Give rest to all (who are) of the Church and give to all mercy and compassion and advancement. We beseech thee on behalf of all who are living as Solitaries (μοναζόντων), and for the Virgins who are keeping their estate (εὖ οὐσῶν). Let them finish their course (2 Tim. iv. 7) unblameably and their life unfailingly, that they may be able to pass through all their days in cleanness and holiness. Have mercy also on all who are married, the men and the women (γύναια) and the children, and give to all a blessing of advancement and improvement, that all may become living and elect men, through thy only-begotten Jesus

[1] It is evident from the absence of Ordination forms for these three classes of "ministers" that they were not ordained in the ordinary sense in the church for which these prayers were collected. There are, indeed, forms for ordaining Subdeacons and Readers, with laying on of hands, in *Apost. Const.* viii. 20—22: see *Int.* § 8, p. 54. But the order to lay hands on them contradicts earlier documents of the same class, e.g. *Can. Hipp.* vii. 48 for Readers, and *Egyptian C.O.* (Lagarde) 36, for Subdeacons. A comparison of Canon 66 of Agde (A.D. 506) with that of Laodicea 21, shows that early in the sixth century Subdeacons (ὑπηρέται) were considered "insacrati ministri." Even in the ninth century Amalarius writes (*De officiis Eccl.* ii. 6) that they do not receive ordination before the altar.

"Interpreters" are rarely mentioned as a separate class. It is natural to find them specially honoured in Egypt, St. Mark being known as the "Interpreter" of St. Peter. Epiphanius (*Expos. fidei*, 21) is quoted as mentioning them, and Procopius the martyr was Reader, Exorcist and Interpreter of the church of Scythopolis in Palestine.

Christ, through whom to thee (is) the glory and the strength both now and to the ages of the ages. Amen.

[PRAYERS OF CONFESSION TO PREPARE THE PEOPLE FOR OFFERING.]

26. *Prayer of bending the knee.*[1]

Father of the only-begotten, good and compassionate, pitiful and lover of men and lover of souls, benefactor of all who turn themselves to thee, receive this supplication, and give us knowledge and faith and piety and holiness. Bring to nought every passion, every lust (ἡδονήν), every sin from (among) this people. Make them all to become clean. Give indulgence to the faults of all. For to thee the uncreated father through the only-begotten do we bend the knee. Give to us a holy understanding and perfect assistance; give to us to seek and to love thee; give to us to search and to seek out thy divine oracles; O Master give to us (thy) hand[2] and raise us up. Raise us up, O God of compassions, cause us to look up. Uncover our eyes, grant us freedom of speech, suffer us not to be ashamed, nor to

---

[1] See *Int.* § 5, pp. 36 and 38 foll.

[2] In Coptic this would simply mean "help us"; but "raise us up" implies a more exact use of the metaphor.

be abashed, nor to accuse (καταγινώσκειν) ourselves. Blot out the bond that is against us
(Coloss. ii. 14). Write our names in the book
of life (*cp*. Philip. iv. 3). Number us together
with thy holy prophets and apostles, through
thy only-begotten Jesus Christ, through whom
to thee (is) the glory and the strength both now
and to all the ages of the ages. Amen.

[PRAYER AND FIXED DIPTYCH ON BEHALF OF
THOSE WHO MAKE OFFERINGS.]

27. Prayer on behalf of (the) people.

A. We may make full confession to thee, O
God who lovest man, and throw before thee our
weaknesses, and beseech thee that strength may
be imparted to us. Pardon our foregone sins
and remit all (our) faults that have passed by
and make (us) new men. Render (δεῖξον) us all
servants of thine own (γνησίους) and clean.
To thee we dedicate ourselves ; receive us, O
God of truth.

[Fixed Diptych.[1]]

B. Receive this people, grant that it may be
entirely thine own. Grant it entirely to walk
unblameably and cleanly. Let them be joined

[1] I have adopted this sub-title on a suggestion of Mr.
Brightman's.

in symmetry (συμμετρηθήτωσαν) with the heavenly ones ; let them be numbered together with the angels ; let them become entirely elect and holy.

We beseech thee on behalf of those who have believed and have come to full knowledge of the Lord Jesus Christ ; let them be confirmed in the faith, and in the knowledge and in the doctrine.

We pray thee on behalf of all this people, be reconciled to all, make thyself known (γνώρισον ἑαυτόν). Reveal thy bright light; let all know thee the uncreated Father and thy only-begotten Son Jesus Christ.

We pray for all Rulers, may they have a peaceable life.[1]

(We pray) for the rest of the Catholic Church.[2]

We pray thee, O God of compassions, for freemen and slaves, males and women, old men and children, poor and rich ; display to all thine own special good, and stretch forth on all thine own special loving-kindness ; have compassion on all and grant to all to turn to thee.

We beseech thee for those who are travelling

---

[1] On the bearing of this petition on the date, see *Int.*, § 2, p. 13.

[2] ὑπὲρ ἀναπαύσεως τῆς καθολικῆς ἐκκλησίας. This *may* be connected with what precedes, "for the sake of the rest of the Catholic Church." But I prefer to take it, as in the text, as a separate petition, beginning as usual with ὑπέρ.

from home (ἀποδημούντων),[1] grant them an angel
of peace as their fellow-traveller, that they may
receive no hurt from any one, that they may
finish (διανύσωσιν) their voyage and their travels
(ἀποδημίας) in much cheerfulness.

We beseech thee for those who are afflicted
and in bonds and in poverty; give rest to each,
free (them) from bonds, bringing (them) out of
poverty; comfort all, thou who art the comforter
and consoler.

We pray for the sick, grant (them) health and
raise (them) up from their sickness, and make
them to have perfect health of body and soul:
for thou art the Saviour and benefactor, thou art
the Lord and King of all.

We have besought thee on behalf of all
through thy only-begotten Jesus Christ,
through whom to thee (is) the glory and the
strength in holy Spirit both now and to all the
ages of the ages. Amen.

[The Offertory doubtless followed here.]

---

[1] ἀποδημεῖν not only means "to be absent from home,"
but ἀπό in this group of words often implies motion, like
ἐπί in ἐπιδημεῖν. *Cp.* Aristophanes *Ranae*, 48, ποῖ γῆς
ἀπεδήμεις;

[BENEDICTIONS TO BE SAID IN CONNECTION WITH PREVIOUS PRAYERS.]

28.[1] *Laying on of hands (Benediction) of Catechumens.*

We stretch out the hand, O Master, and pray that the divine and living hand may be stretched out in blessing on this people. For to thee, uncreated Father, through the only-begotten they have bowed their heads. Bless this people unto (εἰς) the blessing of knowledge and piety, unto the blessing of thy mysteries, through thy only-begotten Jesus Christ, through whom to thee (is) the glory and the strength in holy Spirit both now and to all the ages of the ages. Amen.

29. *Laying on of hands (Benediction) of the laity.*

May the living and clean hand, the hand of the only-begotten, that hath destroyed all evil things and confirmed and established all holy

[1] On χειροθεσία see *Int.* § 8, p. 52 foll., and § 9, p. 56, and Cotelier's note, *Ap. Const.* viii. 9, on the Benediction of Penitents. For similar usages see Mr. Brightman's *Glossary* to his *Liturgies*, s. v. "Imposition of the hand," p. 578. Very probably the different parties came round to the Bishop before they left the church, or as he was leaving it. So Silvia, *Peregrinatio*, frequently has the phrase, "ad manum episcopi acceditur," or the like. (*Cp. Canon. Laod.* 19, quoted *Int.* § 5 ; Silvia *ap.* Duchesne, *Origines*, pp. 471-5, 495 ; *cp.* Brightman, 470, 11.) Traces of this remain here and there, as in the Coptic Church, at Rheims (I think), and at Exeter (for choristers).

things, be stretched out over the heads of this people.   May the people be blessed by the blessing of (the) Spirit, by the blessing of heaven, by the blessing of prophets and apostles. May the bodies of the people be blessed to temperance and cleanness.   May their souls be blessed to learning and knowledge and the mysteries.   May they be blessed all in common through thy only-begotten Jesus Christ through whom to thee (is) the glory and the strength in holy Spirit, both now and to all the ages of (the) ages.   Amen.

30. *Laying on of hands (Benediction) of sick persons.*

O Lord God of compassions, stretch out thine hand and grant that all the sick may be healed. Grant them to be counted worthy of health. Free them from the sickness which lies upon them.   Let them be healed in the name of thy only-begotten.   May his holy name be to them a medicine for health and soundness, because through him to thee (is) the glory and the strength in holy Spirit both now and to all the ages of the ages.   Amen.

All these prayers are performed before the Offertory prayer.

NOTE ON THE DOGMATIC LETTER.

Then follows a short letter, without author's name or definite address, but intended apparently for a brother or near relative, entitled *Concerning Father and Son*. It occupies just four pages of Wobbermin's edition (pp. 21—25). Its subject is the co-eternity of the Father and the Son (the Word), and it is evidently directed against Arianism, which is, however, only described as "the evil speech of the unlearned" (τὴν τῶν ἀπαιδεύτων δυσφημίαν). The holy Spirit is defined as the "bosom of the Father" referred to in St. John i. 18, and as that "in which are all virtues and powers and energies of the Father," just as in the breast of man are all his powers and virtues, which are enumerated at some length (chap. ii.).

The following books and writers are quoted by name from the New Testament—"The Gospel according to John" (three times), "the most honourable Barnabas the Apostle, surnamed son of consolation, in his epistle" (v. 5), "the sacred apostle in his (letter) to Romans," "the sacred Paul the Apostle in his (letter) to Hebrews," "the honourable divinely inspired Gospel according to Luke," "the sacred Paul the Apostle in his (letter) to Colossians," "the

Apocalypse of John " (i. 8), "the Apostolic word written in the Epistle to Hebrews." The only reference to St. Matthew is to the saying of " the Saviour" about the grain of mustard-seed (Matt. xiii. 31). There are several quotations also from the Old Testament.

On the question whether this letter may be ascribed to Sarapion, see *Int.* § 3, pp. 19—23.

ADDITIONAL NOTE.

The following facts mentioned by Dr. Archibald Robertson in his *Select Writings of St. Athanasius* (Oxford and New York, p. 564 note, 4to, 1892), illustrate the history and the importance of Sarapion, whom he considers "the right-hand man of Athanasius among the Bishops of Egypt." Thmuis is named by Ammianus (xxii. 16, 6) as one of the [four] largest cities of Egypt. Sarapion was head of a community of monks before he became Bishop. His promotion probably took place between 337—339 A.D. In that case he would probably be one of the two Sarapions who signed at Sardica in 343. In 353 he was chosen with others for a delicate and perilous mission to Constantius, which was, however, unsuccessful. He is said to have been living after 368. Athanasius' Letter XII. (A.D. 340?) is also addressed to Sarapion " our fellow-minister."

I. INDEX TO THE INTRODUCTION
AND NOTES

G

II. INDEX OF GREEK WORDS
IN THE PRAYERS

The simple numerals refer to the numbers of the Prayers. Where p. is prefixed it means *page*, generally of the *Introduction*.